KU-354-564

Growing Teams

A Down-to-Earth Approach

Eugene C. Fetteroll Jr.
Glen D. Hoffherr
John W. Moran Jr., Ph.D.

© 1993 GOAL/QPC
All rights reserved. No part of this book may be reproduced in any form or by any electronic or mechanical means, including information storage and retrieval systems, without permission in writing from GOAL/QPC.

GOAL/QPC
2 Manor Parkway
Salem, NH 03079
Toll-free: (800) 643-4316
Phone: (603) 890-8800
Fax: (603) 870-9122
Email: service@goal.com
Internet: www.goalqpc.com

Growing Teams:
A Down-to-Earth Approach
Eugene C. Fetteroll Jr., Glen D. Hoffherr, John W. Moran Jr.

Edited by Francine Oddo
Cover design by Lori Champney
Book design by Judi Glidden

Printed in the United States of America

10 9 8 7 6 5 4

ISBN 1-879364-42-5

Acknowledgements

Many people helped bring this book to press. Thanks go to Judi Glidden for her organization and design skills. To Lori Champney, who took on this project in its midst, for her creativity, humor, and unwavering dedication. To Deborah Crovo, for her enthusiasm, willingness to please, fast work, and trips to the store for ice cream. To Susan Griebel for taking time in her busy schedule to proof the final manuscript of this book. To Francine Oddo for her behind-the-scenes work in transforming a manuscript into a book. To Michael Brassard, for *The Memory Jogger*™. And to Bob King, Executive Director of GOAL/QPC, for his confidence in this project.

About GOAL/QPC

GOAL/QPC, a nonprofit organization established in 1978, is an internationally recognized leader in the study and teaching of Total Quality Management (TQM) as an organizational transformation process. Through GOAL/QPC's combination of research, education, training programs, membership, publications, software, and direct consultations, GOAL/QPC has helped hundreds of organizations to begin a quality management program, isolate improvement opportunities, and support TQM or other transformational efforts.

Contents

Figures and Team Exercises

Figures

Team Exercises: 29 User-Friendly Exercises Designed to Grow Teams

Chapter 8

Chapter 9

Chapter 10

Preface

Growing Teams: A Down-to-Earth Approach is a practical treatment of the skills that people need in any organizational environment to help teams grow. Positive results are the ultimate measure of success. This book is intended to provide managers, supervisors, and team leaders with the proven tools and techniques that they can apply to grow successful teams.

In writing this book, we drew from literally thousands of former coworkers and seminar participants to produce the insights that have been distilled into this book. We realize that while many people have experienced success in developing teams, many others have been less fortunate. It is our goal to provide a collection of both helpful hints and user-friendly exercises that, when used together, will help to ensure the growth of teams.

Many professional colleagues provided significant support in the development of this book, and we are indebted to them for their dedication and friendship. Woven throughout the fabric of this book are specific insights that were shared with us by experienced practitioners because of something that really "worked." This book ties into other GOAL/QPC publications on teams and process improvement (the other publications are *The Team Memory Jogger™*, *The Memory Jogger™*, *The Memory Jogger™ II*, and the *Coach's Guide to The Memory Jogger™ II*), which should serve as the beginning level of daily management for those familiar with the topic.

When we decided to write this book as a team effort, we wanted to use our many years of business experience to produce a working book that was designed to help readers succeed in their organization's teams. We hope that our emphasis on a practical "how-to-do-it" approach will facilitate the implementation and growth of teams, with resulting productivity and human resource benefits.

Introduction

Growing teams is a process to effect a culture change in an organization. Culture is the reflection of an organization's past history. The people in an organization have learned how to behave and adapt in the organization's environment—they learn by observing the behavior of those in positions "above" them in the organization. They manifest their adaptive behavior in ways that are visible to others, such as:

- How they convey knowledge and information
- How they reward and recognize performance
- Their protocol within the organization
- Positive or negative attitudes
- Personal values
- Shared beliefs

The teaming process is a method of involving everyone in the organization to:

- Collaborate
- Build on achieving consensus
- Become aware of the interdependency between people
- Share knowledge
- Be open
- Harness the synergy of collaboration
- Develop ownership and responsibility for action
- Integrate individual needs and goals with those of the organization
- Focus on organizational problems, analyze the problems with the people directly involved, and develop shared solutions that optimize the whole and not one of the parts of the whole

Before an organization adopts teaming as a way of life, the management staff needs to adopt a new attitude and believe that the employees know more about their job functions than they do. The reason it is important to grow teams is that they almost always positively affect the current culture. Initially, employees and executives perceive a culture change as a threat to the status quo. Unfortunately, many organizations begin to form teams without adequate planning and discussion and direction, and then teams produce disappointing results. Many organizations, unsure how to begin implementing improvements, have followed the popular trend of starting teams because other organizations are starting teams. This attempt allows management to state unequivocally that they have tried teams.

Growing teams is an incremental approach to building a foundation for success. Bottom-up teaming will fail. It must be driven, empowered, and lead from the top of the organization. All teams have common growth characteristics such as building trust, learning the art of consensus, learning to work together, and accomplishing tasks to fulfill shared goals.

Introduction

Teams, to be successful, need to form on solid ground: they need a direct purpose, specific goals, and meaningful ways to measure their purpose and goals. Too often organizations begin teams for "teaming sake" rather than to improve the organization and consciously begin to change the culture. This lack of focus on results can frustrate and anger team members and provides little or no benefit to the organization. Experience has shown that these teams tend to have less and less influence over time until they disband.

In the 1920s, Frederick Taylor concluded that management knows what is best for the organization. This philosophy of Taylor's has formed the customary standard of management practice in the United States, squelching the belief that employees can make meaningful contributions to quality. Frederick Taylor was a mechanical engineer in the late nineteenth century who joined a factory as a lathe hand and worked his way up to manager of the machine shop. It was at this time that dramatic changes in social and economic structures worldwide were taking place—better known as the Industrial Revolution. Inventions and new technology had created the factory system of large-scale machine production, changing economies from laborer-intensive to economies that relied less on laborers and strongly on machines. Taylor believed that the foremen and workers of those days lacked the educational qualifications to decide how work should be done, what constituted a day's work, or how to select and train workers. As a result of his belief, Taylor set out to change the shop organization. He created positions for specialists to plan the work, and relegated the foremen and workers to executing the work plans, in effect, separating planning from doing.

The work world, fortunately, has been changing. The adoption of a team culture is a cumulative building process that begins with organizational need and ends with a new culture in which everyone participates to their capability. To do this, you need to involve people. Throughout history, the people doing the work in the workplace have had the best ideas on how to improve their own processes. In the last century, the message that management has been sending is "We don't want your ideas, check your mind at the door. You are being paid to do a job, not to think." People are usually hired to accomplish a specific function. Traditionally, the function was broken down more narrowly until every individual had only one specific job. As a result of this buildup of culture over the years, many people continue to avoid offering ideas to improve their processes, for fear of punishment or *indifference*. Management continues to dominate rather than lead. The focus on the customer continues to diminish and the focus on the organization becomes prevalent. Management will have more success if they give the proper credit and encouragement to those who practice teamwork and who are willing to share ideas and new, more effective ways of accomplishing their jobs.

When management develops a team culture and gradually grows teams, the people of an organization are encouraged to share their ideas with the team. Processes are improved by the most knowledgeable individuals. This team nurturing initially provides a feeling of safety through numbers. A team that presents an improvement idea has more clout than an individual.

An individual, acting as part of a team, may feel safer in revealing ideas that are potentially different culturally than proposing such ideas outside the context of the team. This growing and nurturing of teams requires an effort to change years of inertia on the part of management to accept everyone's input and stimulus to change.

There are numerous types of teams and they are called by any number of names. Each team needs to understand why their team exists. By understanding the purpose of the team, each member can contribute fully. Described below are some of the common types of teams that are formed.

Worker Teams. These teams are comprised of employees at the same general level (for example, quality circles). These teams frequently bond tightly, but they have to overcome obstacles as they attempt to create change outside their sphere of influence. Many of these teams must continue to deal within the current corporate culture, which often does not fully support teaming concepts.

Functional Teams. Many of these teams follow the current organizational structures found in most organizations today. These teams fall within the "stovepipe," or departmental hierarchy, of their own functional area, such as engineering, manufacturing, sales, accounting, and so forth. These teams often fall prey to the traditional power struggles within their organization.

Process-Action Teams. These are cross-functional teams that are focused on a critical process that intersects the traditional stovepipes (departmental hierarchies) of the organization. The initial forming sessions these teams go through are often difficult to focus and frustrating for members, however, the resulting benefits of the team's synergy, created by the diverse viewpoints of members, is well worth the time and organizational effort.

Steering Teams. Cross-functional teams at the top levels of the organization. They usually focus on strategies and critical organizational systems. These teams often take much longer to form as a team because there are usually strong forces between the personalities of the team members.

Teamwork can help to overcome broader cultural issues that are affecting the workplace—issues of literacy, for example. There are two major barriers inhibiting literacy; one is the language barrier, and the other is education. The strength of the team as a well-functioning unit can help other members to overcome these barriers and encourage valuable members of the work force to contribute to the well-being of their organizations.

The team idea in the workplace is relatively new, and still a foreign one to many people because it is not the cornerstone of our educational system. Children and teenagers have not been encouraged to work with their classmates in school or outside of school, and so many people have worked through school as individuals, were graded as individuals, and have learned to advance in the business world as individuals. The feat of bringing people together to work as a team is an accomplishment by itself, and requires of all the members that they never stop looking for ways to build, develop, and grow their team, lest their team process fail. Teams need to begin with easy successes and then build on those successes.

The process of growing teams incorporates numerous areas including training, providing recognition for team achievements, ensuring credit is given to the team on a continual basis for team accomplishments, and looking for ways to continuously improve the way the team feels about its accomplishments, failures, and challenges they are working to resolve.

Growing teams starts at the very beginning, is a continual process, and is designed to make teams as strong (and flexible) as possible, maximizing each member's self-esteem. This nurturing provides teams with the greatest opportunity to produce positive results.

Basic Instructions for Leading the Exercises

You are about to begin a journey that will take you through 29 user-friendly exercises that are designed to grow teams and involve each member of the team. The exercises are simple to use but yield illuminating discoveries.

Each exercise is carefully designed, using a proven format that will enable you to spend your time learning and sharing, as opposed to interpreting directions. In each case the exercise begins with the title and a clear statement of **purpose** so you will know right away if this exercise is fit for you and/or your team. To keep the process efficient, detailed **preparation** points are listed to help you plan your time.

Next is a clear explanation of the **process**. This explanation lets you know exactly what the participants completing the exercise need to do, coupled with a realistic estimate of the time required to accomplish it.

The last phase of each exercise is **discussion**. Step-by-step guidelines are provided that will enable the person leading the exercise to extract all the valuable learning that is built into the exercise. The discussion phase of the exercise is designed to give the leader considerable flexibility with time. For example, if you are low on time, you can eliminate one or more discussion steps. If you have more time than you planned, you can extend the discussion by allowing more input from the participants.

Three guidelines round out the instructions for these very practical exercises.

▶ **Time Required:** This estimate is based on practical experience. Both the minimum and maximum time requirements are noted.

▶ **Group Size:** An optimum number of participants is between 4 and 9. In some cases the group may be larger, but it should not be larger than 20 participants.

▶ **Prepare Participants:** Ask individuals to share their responses with the group. The more honest and forthright their answers, the more beneficial these chapter exercises are to the participants and their organization.

Chapter 1
Understanding Your Organization

Key Points

- What is the culture you work in?
- Two assessment tools
- Now, what is it you want to change?

Before organizations can start to grow teams, they need to assess from where they are starting. They need to establish a baseline from which they can measure their progress. This chapter discusses some of the cultural aspects of change in organizations that have decided to use teams.

Beliefs and Behaviors

Growing teams requires organizations to focus on what they want to change. Change is usually met with resistance. One of the primary reasons for this resistance is that change forces people to recognize and modify behaviors that are habitual; behaviors that people don't even think about. Have you ever tried to stop smoking, drinking, or eating too much? The capacity to unlearn a behavior that has been repeated and rewarded for years or decades, even when you are strongly self-motivated, can be overwhelming. You may smoke fewer cigarettes, drink less, or sneak high-calorie snacks instead of eating them in front of others, but you still resist changing.

Teaming is usually resisted because it is foreign to our learned culture, our way of organizational life, our reward system, and our work environment.

The culture that has been established in an organization depicts the image the organization wants to portray. Culture is not tangible, but surrounds us. It influences our decision process, (what is acceptable, what is not), and it is so pervasive that we don't often recognize it or its impact. Culture is a combination of people, systems, structures, working space, facilities, beliefs, values, and prejudices.

Culture is built up over years and it takes a significant amount of time, discipline, and persistence to change it. Organizations can begin to understand their work cultures by thinking of the elements that guide their day-to-day behavior. Having worked with numerous beginning teams, we took the opportunity to ask them what elements they believe exist in their work culture.

Some examples teams list as elements of their culture are:

- Autocratic behavior
- People are the problem
- Product out versus customer satisfaction
- Bottom-line results are the only measure
- People react on feelings not data
- People work too many long hours
- Organization is in constant state of flux

One way to assess an organization's culture is to enumerate on a balance sheet the positive and negative aspects of the organization (see Figure 1-1).

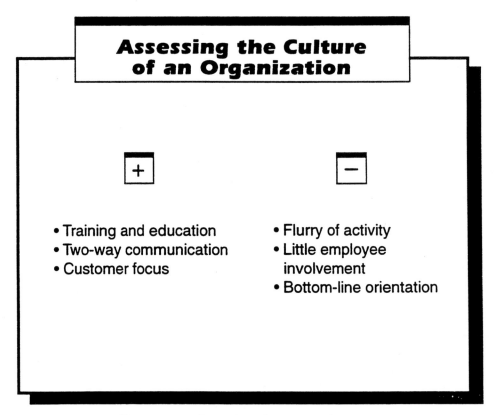

Figure 1-1 Balance Sheet of Good
and Bad of Organization

Another way to assess an organization's culture is to ask everyone to complete a survey. The responses of the survey can then be summarized to create a baseline of how the culture is perceived by employees currently. An example of this type of survey is shown in Figure 1-2. By looking at the responses of the survey, two different assessments can be made: 1) the current culture can be defined and 2) teams can choose the areas in the organization that need improvement. From here, organizations can work toward creating a vision of how they would like their cultures to look.

When organizations understand from where they are starting, they can set goals for the change they want to achieve. Once they are clear on the extent of the change they want, they can then grow teams to accomplish change.

Assessing the Culture of an Organization

	SD	D	A	SA
1. Employee input is valued and solicited.	—	—	—	—
2. We have a collaborative environment.	—	—	—	—
3. We have an ongoing, continual improvement process.	—	—	—	—
4. We have a clear direction, goals, and the appropriate resources to accomplish our mission.	—	—	—	—

KEY
SD = strongly disagree
D = disagree
A = agree
SA = strongly agree

Figure 1-2 What Would the Organization Look Like
with a New Culture?

We stress a growing process, not a starting process. Growing requires nurturing, monitoring, helping, whereas, a starting process involves launching a team but does not provide for the continual progress of a team. One aspect of the growing process that is often overlooked is the part of the process that falls onto the team itself. As team members begin relying more on each other, they are less apt to blame one another for things that go wrong. This evolution also entails team members to give credit where it is appropriate.

Another aspect of the growing process is management and the feedback that the team receives from management. The growing of the team is internal to the team itself. Support comes from management. Because of this duality, a good baseline is essential to allow teams to focus their energy and self-management in beginning to look at the areas most in need of change.

The support of management helps the team process, but teams must accept the responsibility for their own growth and development. If teams do not have a real desire to be successful, nothing can force them to be.

The following exercise is designed to allow you to assess the culture of your organization as it currently exists. Complete the questions honestly. There are no wrong answers. The results should be plotted and checked periodically to measure how well the organization is progressing toward its goals in its growth of a team culture. A radar chart will work well for plotting your results. A radar chart is a tool that can be used to record a group's assessment of the organization's culture. The measurement scale can be either quantitative or qualitative.

quantitative

qualitative

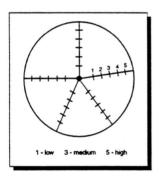

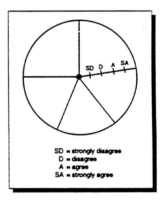

Each spoke projecting from the center of the radar chart represents one of the measurement criteria chosen. The scale of measurement is set up so that the farther from the center, the better the score. For more discussion on baselining and radar charts, see Chapter 1 of *Making Daily Management Work: A Perspective for Leaders and Managers.*

This page is intentionally left blank.

Exercise 1 Instructions

What is the Culture in Your Organization?

Purpose
Certain behaviors and activities have been identified as crucial to the growth and development of teams in any organization. In this exercise, participants review fifteen statements and then use a rating scale to indicate the extent to which each behavior or activity is present in their workplace.

Preparation
- Give each participant a copy of the exercise.
- Provide enough pens and pencils for everyone.
- Lay out several multicolored felt tip markers for anyone to use.
- Set up a flip chart or writing board in the area.

Process
- Ask participants to read each statement in Exercise 1. Encourage them to complete the exercise by following their "gut" or initial response to each statement. Instruct participants to circle the number that they believe most closely represents the extent to which the statement is true in the culture of their organization. A "1" indicates that the behavior or activity described never occurs, and a "5" means it always occurs.
- Allow 5 minutes for participants to complete the exercise.

Discussion
- Review each statement one by one. Poll the group to get a rough idea of how the participants rated each item.
- On statements that were rated low, use group discussion to generate ideas for strengthening the described behavior or activity.
- On statements that were rated high, use group discussion to generate ideas for maintaining the described behavior or activity.
- Close the discussion by identifying which behaviors and activities that, if developed more fully throughout the organization, can have the most positive effect on the culture of the organization.

▶ Time required: 60–90 minutes total
▶ Group size: Optimum is 4–9 people, but up to 20 people is acceptable

Exercise 1
What is the Culture in Your Organization?

Take this survey and find out.

Circle the number that you believe most closely represents the extent to which the statement is true in the culture of your organization. A "1" indicates that the behavior or activity described never occurs, and a "5" means it always occurs.

1 When conflict occurs among team members, it is dealt with openly.

     1   2   3   4   5

2 Proven problem-solving techniques are used. (Flowcharts, cause and effect diagrams, Pareto charts, and so forth.)

     1   2   3   4   5

3 Activities are provided to help people learn more about the organization.

     1   2   3   4   5

4 Teams have ground rules to help all members do their part in keeping meetings on track.

     1   2   3   4   5

5 People may say "Team meetings are fun."

     1   2   3   4   5

6 Every team member has an opportunity to share in the leadership of the meetings.

     1   2   3   4   5

7 People really make an effort to listen to each other.

     1   2   3   4   5

Exercise 1

8 Effort is made to ensure that individuals will be comfortable when they participate.

      1   2   3   4   5

9 Every team member understands what brainstorming means and it is used effectively.

      1   2   3   4   5

10 Customer expectations are communicated clearly to team members.

      1   2   3   4   5

11 Team members are genuinely involved and believe that they do "make a difference."

      1   2   3   4   5

12 Training has been provided throughout the organization in all aspects of growing teams.

      1   2   3   4   5

13 Continuous constructive feedback is provided in all team meetings.

      1   2   3   4   5

14 Specific and attainable goals are set by the members of the team.

      1   2   3   4   5

15 The level of trust among team members is high.

      1   2   3   4   5

Chapter 2
Management's Role in the Team Process

Key Points

- Benefits for management in growing teams
- Wanted: seven commitments from management

Managers' roles and responsibilities in the team growing process are critical. Management is the key to making or breaking the team process. It is not what is said, but what is done by the entire management staff that results in a team thriving, growing, or withering. The outgrowth of cultural change to a team environment produces a change in the ways business is performed and management's role changes to a leadership role.

How Can Management Benefit from Growing Teams?

Management needs to provide a supportive environment with high expectations for the team. There are numerous benefits to the organization by tapping the team's potential. Many managers are at first fearful of the team approach, since they have been successful for a number of years demonstrating the very skills they are now being asked to change, such as fire fighting, working as individual contributors, and assuming major responsibility. In addition, as the team culture becomes real over time, many of the managers' current functions will disappear.

Some of the benefits of growing teams that may help alleviate management's fears include:

- **Team members will lend more support to a team-focused organization than individuals working independently.** When people are part of a team, they will provide support for the team, which will result in higher productivity and increased quality.

- **Communication will be more open.** The result of more open communication is that new ideas will be voiced, problems will be identified earlier and resolved more easily, and organizations will operate more effectively.

- **Team results will provide recognition for all involved.** When the team does well, associated management will receive residual benefits that include personal kudos and other forms of rewards and recognition.

- **Success breeds success.** As teams are initially successful, others will begin to emulate their practices, and the organization's culture will continue to change.

What is Management's Commitment to the Team Process?

Management is often starting fresh with the concept of teams. One of the first decisions that management needs to make is whether the organization is ready for teams and whether it is willing to accept the recommendations for improvements from the teams. If management is uncertain that it is willing to accept responsibility for the following seven roles of team commitment, it should not begin the team process. These roles are:

1. Empowerment
2. Delegation
3. Motivation
4. Training
5. Coaching
6. Participation
7. Leadership

1 & 2: Managers as Delegators and a Source of Empowerment

Empowerment entails many factors that include participation, power, permission, protection, parameters, and willingness to accept responsibility. (More on this in Chapter 6.) For managers who are not yet comfortable with empowering teams to function independently, it will be a challenge for them to relinquish some authority in allowing teams to suggest and make changes, and to provide teams with protection from failure or retribution. Both of these characteristics are a shift from the cultural norm many managers are accustomed to, but are necessary for fostering the success of teams.

Empowering others requires a special focus by managers. Managers should ask themselves the following questions:

When I empower a team, to what extent do I focus on the desired end results rather than on the specific steps team members take to accomplish those result?

To what extent do team members have the freedom to develop their own means to carry out assigned tasks and projects?

To what extent do I allow the team to make important decisions on its own?

To what extent do I encourage the team to solve its own problems, and do I resist the urge to offer solutions?

To what extent am I able to keep my hands out of the team's day-to-day activities?

To what extent do team members fully understand the nature and the scope of what I have delegated to them?

Have I provided the team with the necessary resources?

Do team members understand the level of authority they have to carry out their tasks?

How well does the team understand the ground rules within which it can perform?

Have I worked out an effective reporting process with team members regarding their responsibilities?

To what extent do I encourage the team to exercise self-direction and self-control?

To what extent do team members have control over what they do, and how they do it?

How will I need to change myself to be able to contribute to changing the culture of the organization from its present state to one that supports the teaming process?

3: Managers as Motivators

Management plays another key role. The role of motivator. Even though managers are not normally active participants on teams, their role as motivators is needed. There are many, many ways to motivate people, listed below is a sampling of ten techniques that managers can use to gain the trust and confidence of team members.

1.   Let team members know their contributions are important and are required for the success of the team.
2.   Inform the team of any changes in corporate strategies as soon as you are able.
3.   Earn the confidence, loyalty, and trust of team members by displaying team culture behavior.
4.   Understand each team member. Find out about the team members' interests, habits, sensitive areas, preferred problem-solving methods, and then use this knowledge to provide the resources required to make the best use of their strengths.
5.   Understand that mistakes are learning experiences, not a basis to point blame.
6.   Set the style of acceptable performance characteristics in the group.
7.   Demonstrate pride and confidence in the team at every opportunity.
8.   Diffuse potential problems as they occur. Keep personal feelings out of the team environment.
9.   Provide positive feedback, reward, and recognize team performance whenever possible.
10. Keep your team informed of what is going on.

4: Managers as Supporters of Training and Team Growth

In nurturing the development of teams, managers will want to give support, that is re-sources *not* lip service, to providing training for team members so teams may work to-gether better. This chapter focuses on the team training that managers should participate in and provide for their teams. Depending on how many team members have participated on other teams, the amount of training time we recommend may not apply. The amount of time we recommend for each type of training is purely a guideline for people who have little or no experience participating on teams.

Group Dynamics Training. This is the human side of the teaming process. Members learn how to act, interact, and relate in group situations and contexts. Most initial teams spend a minimum of four hours training in human dynamics.

Process Methodologies Training. This involves the processes that teams will use to work on improving a process or fixing a problem. There are numerous models to accom-plish this, however, we feel strongly that the model should include the areas covered in the twelve-step model for process improvement, which is presented in Chapter 8. Initial teams usually spend at least four hours defining the methodology they will use for the first pro-cess.

Tools Training. Depending on the process methodology, the number and type of tools used will vary dramatically. Initial tools training is most effective when it is performed on a just-in-time basis. Managers or team leaders should be proficient in using the tools to be able to suggest the right tool at the right time, and to be available as a source for follow-up training.

Preferred-Thinking-Styles Training. Many managers may choose to overlook this type of training. However, it can provide a great deal of additional information for team mem-bers and help them value each another's differences. If this type of training is provided, it can be accomplished in four to eight hours. (For information on two popular tools used to assess a person's preferred thinking style, *see* explanations of the Herrmann Brain Domi-nance Profile and the Meyers-Briggs Personality Profile in Appendix A.

Roles and Responsibilities. The various roles and responsibilities of the team members should be explained in the team selection process or in the first team meeting. This nor-mally takes less than one hour and provides a structure and groundwork for the team's upcoming tasks.

5: Managers as Coaches

As coaches, managers will need to be cheerleaders, parent figures, motivators, process experts, and customers! (More on coaching in Chapter 3.)

6: Managers as Participants

Managers may also be asked to participate on teams. These teams will be cross-functional and within their own division. Managers should *exemplify the same qualities that they expect other team members to exhibit.* (More on the roles of managers and team members in Chapter 4.)

7: Managers as Leaders

One of the greatest tasks that managers will be asked to do is become leaders of the teaming process. We believe there are some qualities common in all good leaders. Good leaders:

1. **Guide and instruct others.** Leaders must point the way for new directions and ideas. In return for helping others achieve success, they can derive pleasure and deep satisfaction from knowing they were instrumental in a team's success.
2. **Think about others first.** They are sensitive to other people's feelings and genuinely care about them.
3. **Know the people on the team.** Leaders know team members individually and what motivates them. Leaders take the time to get acquainted with those who work with them.
4. **Communicate clearly.** They do not try to impress others with superficial language or try to make others believe they know what they are talking about when they really do not. They speak in a straightforward manner and are easy to understand.
5. **Listen.** They listen to others. They hear concerns and are willing to be told of tragedies as well as triumphs. They enjoy hearing the voices and insights of others.
6. **Promote stability.** They know that peace, growth, and prosperity come from a stable environment. They accept change as a way to achieve stability.
7. **Think before acting.** They know they are responsible for the welfare of others. They care about how a situation will affect all those concerned. They learn the facts before taking action.
8. **Strive to learn continually.** Leaders devour information and enjoy learning. They read books, ask questions, are open to new ideas, get involved, and have a *thirst* to understand other people, situations, events, and phenomenon.
9. **Value honesty.** Leaders are honest and ask the same of others. They do not mislead or hide the facts. They admit their mistakes openly.
10. **Seek challenges.** Leaders look for bigger and more interesting mountains to climb and lead their followers toward new horizons. Leaders can thrive during tough times.

Managers who accept the responsibility of these seven roles will be a catalyst in creating a successful team culture. Without management's care and nurturing, teams will start and fail. With careful attention from management, however, teams can grow and help their organization to prosper.

After managers address these seven roles among themselves and with team members, they are ready to commit to a contract with the team. The contracting process, which includes negotiation, provides the team and management with a clear definition of the scope of the team's responsibilities, desired outcomes, resources, time allotted, and boundaries of the process being addressed. The contracting process is often the first step in changing the corporate climate to support teams.

It is very reasonable to have high expectations for teams. These expectations can be attained successfully if they are defined in the contracting process. If expectations are not defined, they can never be met. Just as in all other aspects of life, if the destination is unknown, any road you take will get you there.

Management must ensure during the contracting process that its role of coach and mentor, *not superior and boss*, is defined and understood by the team and is clear to the leaders themselves. Management needs to understand the impact and ramifications of putting teams into place before the organization embarks on the path of growing teams.

This page is intentionally left blank.

Exercise 2 Instructions

How Can Team Building Help Managers?

Purpose

Managers are usually extremely busy, and for this reason they may fail to consider all of the advantages that a team effort can produce. This exercise gives participants ten possible advantages of team performance. Participants are asked to mark an "x" in the box that precedes each statement if they believe the statement would be of value in the process of growing and developing teams in their work areas.

Preparation

- Give each participant a copy of the exercise.
- Provide enough pens and pencils for everyone.
- Lay out several multicolored felt tip markers for anyone to use.
- Set up a flip chart or writing board in the area.

Process

- Ask participants to read the statements in Exercise 2. Participants should select the statements they believe would be valuable to growing and developing teams in their work areas. Participants should mark an "x" in the box that appears in front of the statement. Don't look for right or wrong answers, there aren't any.
- Allow 4 minutes for participants to complete the exercise.

Discussion

- Review each statement one by one. Ask for a show of hands to see how many people selected each statement. Post the number on a flip chart.
- As each statement is discussed, ask one or two people who selected it to explain why. This will stimulate thinking in other members of the group.
- If no one selected a given statement, ask the group for any ideas on how the statement might provide an advantage to team building.

▶ Time required: 60–75 minutes total
▶ Group size: Optimum is 4–9 people, but up to 20 people is acceptable

Exercise 2
How Can Team Building Help Managers?

Time: 4 minutes

A checklist to help you define your personal methods for self-improvement and team growth.

Some advantages of team performance are listed below. Select the statements you believe would be valuable to growing and developing teams in your work area. Mark an "x" in the box that appears in front of the statement.

❑ **1** Team members who understand each others' priorities will provide help when problems arise.

❑ **2** Communication of new ideas, improved work methods, problems, and other concerns is encouraged.

❑ **3** Feedback on job performance is more meaningful because team members understand what is expected.

❑ **4** Recognition is given to teams for outstanding results, as well as to individuals for personal contributions.

❑ **5** Employees and managers give each other mutual support.

❑ **6** Working effectively as a team in one department is good preparation for working as a team with other departments.

❑ **7** Since team members contribute to the development of department goals, these goals, most likely, are realistic and attainable.

❑ **8** Problem solving is more effective because the entire team can contribute to the solution. The result is "people support what they help to create."

❑ **9** Conflict is more likely to be resolved quickly when team members discuss it openly.

❑**10** Employees are encouraged to try new ideas, knowing that not all ideas will succeed.

NOTES

Chapter 3
Beginning Teams

Key Points

- How does team size affect creativity, trust, communication, and performance?
- What is the ideal team size?
- Three important elements for growing teams
- 16 guidelines for teams to work effectively

There are any number of ways to start teams, however, growing teams is significantly more difficult. Organizations that start teams can tell you exactly how many teams they have and how many people are involved with them. Organizations that grow teams will have no idea of how many teams are functioning at any given time. Organizations will know that teams are able to improve their job functions and have the ability and drive to improve their processes.

Start Strong

Many organizations start teams by convening a group of individuals that have something in common (they may all do the same type of job) and give them the directive to "go fix it" or "improve what you do." As has been proven time and time again, this method is doomed to failure. Not only is it expensive, it is frequently demoralizing and if done in the guise of continual improvement, sows the seeds of failure.

A significant advantage of instilling a team culture is that management helps to foster a culture of cooperation. When a team culture is being grown, people are much less apt to blame others, since in effect, they would be blaming themselves. Teams are able to benefit from the wealth of ideas that different people can bring to the table. Employees see the opportunity, within a team, to voice their ideas and get assistance in expanding on them. Teams provide a basis for real synergy. In growing teams, "crazy" ideas are accepted, explored, and expanded on, piggybacked onto other ideas and made workable and productive. The team culture increases the opportunity for better solutions, not just more of them.

Before teams initially form, their purpose should be developed by their sponsors. Team sponsors are individuals that "own" the process at issue or the organization. If sponsors have the authority to make and implement changes to processes, then they "own" them. Sponsors should be available to help teams establish goals, objectives, and measures of the team's success. Organizations should select initial teams very carefully. At times it is acceptable to use volunteers on the team, however, it may be necessary, for technical or practical reasons, to increase the number of team members for a longer period of time.

How do organizations determine the best size for each team? The following paragraphs are from an article titled "Team Size?" from QLP News, The New England Newsletter of the Quality Leadership Process, and is reprinted with permission from the author and editor, Norman W. Young.

What is the right size team for optimum performance, for learning, for creativity, and for problem solving? There are at least as many answers to this question as there are people and situations. Consulting the "experts" both within and outside the quality movement yields no consistent final answer but does provide a number of basic principles that can guide us to building right-sized teams.

Sigmund Freud taught that "groups form to satisfy individual needs," and Schultz's Fundamental Interpersonal Relations Orientation defines the three needs of individuals in groups as *inclusion, affection, and control.* We know from our training and experience that there is a process through which groups must move before they will begin to form into a team. This process of forming, storming, norming, and performing is highly dependent on communication between individuals in the team. During this process, *communication* is the vehicle that facilitates individual role definition within the team (a person may serve different roles in different teams), and to develop the trust, integrity, and intimacy that allows each person's basic needs to be met. Each individual communication takes time. In fact, it is easy to reach a point where the only work being performed by a team is the interaction necessary to sustain its existence. Full team concentration on a team goal is dependent on the satisfaction of individual needs.

A factor bearing directly on the time required for a team to reach the level of "performing" is the teaming experience of the team members. When a group of people are brought together who have learned and successfully applied the teaming skills of dialogue, brainstorming, questioning, and listening, in other team situations, they are generally quicker to pass through the phases to an acceptable level of performance. They are less threatened by the open interaction that must take place, and barring other complications, move together quickly. Hence, larger teams can be accommodated within the same time constraints. When dealing with teams that are in the skill development stage (training), smaller is better, allowing time for the full exploration and resolution of team-building issues and development of the requisite skills.

Closely bound to the skills of the team members is the composition of the team and its suitability to the project undertaken by the team. Diversity is a key to team creativity and the potential for breakthrough thinking. It is vital that old paradigms be broken for new ones to be forming. This progression of a team is often defined as multilevel and multifunctional. However, it is critical that the team have "expertise" in key process areas as well as diversity. William Byham, author of *ZAPP! The Lightning of Empowerment* suggests letting team members select and expand the team as they see fit to meet the goals of the team.

It should be further noted that any additions to a team sets the team back and causes the team to revisit earlier phases of team development in order to assimilate the newcomer. It is clearly less upsetting if the team has made the selection of the new individual, as they will be prepared to accept the change. Changes forced on a team from an external source are most devastating.

Who or what determines the right size of a team? There are at least three key factors:

- How much *time* is available to allow vital communication to occur and trust to build.
- What *skills* each team member brings to the team.
- What the goal or project is that the team is working to complete.

Teams are constantly changing and growing, and it is vital to recognize the dynamic nature of teams.

Finally consider these thoughts. Team creativity grows as team size (and diversity) increase. The factors of skill level and leadership certainly can extend the productive size of a team, however, at some point the creativity gives way to confusion, and creativity drops. Similarly, as the size of a team grows, it becomes ever more difficult to reach consensus. In Figure 3-1, a team size of 5 or 6 people is indicated as the ideal size. This graph is not from a scientific study but from experiential observation. Observe teams in your environment. Consider the factors that influence team size. The right size of teams will stand out through their performance.

—Norman W. Young

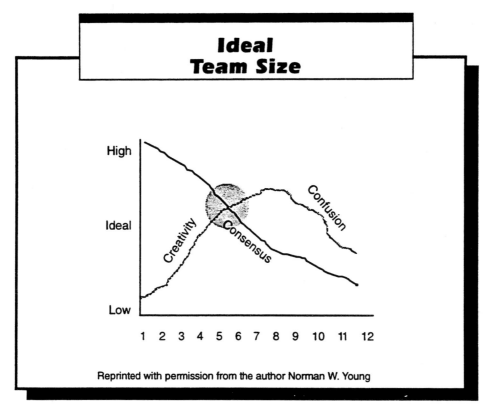

Figure 3-1 Ideal Number of People on a Team

Teams provide a vehicle to discover better ways to do things, ways that are less costly, and ways that better meet the needs of the organization's or team's customers. When these new approaches are developed through the people who are doing the jobs, a wonderful phenomenon kicks in. People support what they helped to create. The people who had the ideas that have moved to the stage of being implemented will work very hard to ensure that the implementation is successful. As members of the organization observe other people's ideas being implemented, they will work more effectively and be more dedicated to making their own ideas work, as well as the ideas of others. Organizations can only benefit by having ideas for improvement that are generated more frequently and implemented more quickly, efficiently, and effectively at the lowest possible level of the organization. Teams become true owners of ideas and virtually all members work harder for something they own, rather than something they have little or no control over.

The team structure provides people with an approach to work together in overcoming communication barriers, which often have negative effects on the operations of the organization.

Members of the team have an opportunity to contribute in a sharing atmosphere. The strengths of each member of the team can be built on enabling people to learn faster in a supportive environment. Differences in problem-solving approaches can be examined using the Herrmann Brain Dominance Profile (see Appendix A) or the Meyers-Briggs Type Indicator (see Appendix A). This knowledge of our team co-members can have a very positive impact on the dynamics of the team.

Team members need to do several things to continue their self-development. One of them is to read. They should avail themselves of libraries to find articles, videotapes, and books that have been written about teams and how teams are successful. This will help them gain an understanding of the entire team process. There are additional sources of information in trade journals, newspapers, congressional papers and so forth.

Another area of opportunity for team members is to participate in selected courses, seminars, or programs offered at their company, high schools, or local community colleges.

Three Important Elements for Growing Teams

Element 1
Coaching. The team process, if started in the normal fashion of forcing it onto the organization, can have more negative impact than positive. It can cause a lack of productivity on the part of the team members. They may feel that ownership has been taken away and management is bulldozing them, and their opportunity for personal accomplishment is greatly diminished.

In organizations that are growing teams, coaching is a key requirement. Coaches allow teams to retain ownership by seeking ways to enhance team ideas, build on them, and not look for change for the sake of change. The idea of coaching teams is to provide suggestions, not to tell teams what to do. This is a fine but critical difference. Coaches may be managers, supervisors, from human resources, coworkers, or other knowledgeable individuals.

The role of the coach is not to tell people what they have done wrong and how to correct it, but to provide knowledge and assistance when problems with the team process are encountered.

Element 2
Allowing the team to grow through mistakes. No one wants to make a mistake that is going to cause injury to a person, that will damage the customer/supplier relationship, or negatively affect quality or delivery. However, there are many cases where teams can be given sufficient leeway to try something. The team must be allowed a certain amount of time, money, and other resources to try out something. If it does not work as expected, that is okay. If it does, that may be even better, although, sometimes more is learned in failed efforts than successful ones.

Letting a team grow through mistakes, rather than just telling members it won't work allows the team to gain knowledge and confidence. This process can be painful to observe at times. Many people have tried certain things unsuccessfully and want to share their knowledge in an attempt to shorten the development time for a team. This often produces an unwanted effect on the team. Allowing them to learn for themselves builds team unity.

Element 3
Facilitating the team so members can work together. There are numerous reasons why teams become dysfunctional. They include:

- *Lack of training* – This lack of training includes training on team processes, interpersonal relationships, use of tools, and so forth.
- *Individuals singled out for recognition* – Recognition of a specific individual from someone outside of the team is often the basis for problems within the team. This frequently causes team members to believe that the person being recognized is "stealing the thunder" and team members hesitate to continue to contribute.
- *Tendency to place blame* – In the early stages, teams often attempt to assess or place blame instead of focusing on the process.

Before organizations start growing teams, they should investigate these questions:

- What is team building?
- Who is involved?
- What process should be used?
- What is the benefit for the team leader?
- Why would employees want to be part of the team?
- What are some tips on setting up a team?

As teams continue to grow, team sponsors and leaders should take care to nurture them. This means:

- Coaching the team, *not* dictating it
- Allowing team members to grow through mistakes
- Understanding why some team members may not work well together
- Keeping communication open

Preventive maintenance is required to keep teams running effectively. Questions that teams should address (and revisit) include:

- How does the team assess its process and problem-solving aptitude?
- What are the behaviors and beliefs of effective team builders?
- What conditions need to be met for teams to work at an optimum?
- What will help team members to focus on the task at hand and not on each other?
- Will the team have an impact on the organization? What kind?
- What are the career implications for the team leader?

- How can team members keep their meetings focused on achieving outcomes and investigating problems rather than just having a good time?

To ensure that teaming becomes an integral part of an organization's culture, proper rewards and recognition must become routine. Some questions for your team to consider include:

- What is the role of recognition for team performance?
- Will recognizing and rewarding a team for its performance have an impact on the team's performance in the future? On other teams? What kind of impact?
- Will employees who do not participate on a team fear they will lose their individual power?

Team members will have a better chance at growing together as a team and breaking down their task at hand if they receive specialized training on problem solving. Training team members to use planning and problem-solving tools and techniques will help them in their mission. Some of these tools and techniques are:

- Bar Graph and Pie Chart
- Brainstorming
- Cause and Effect Diagram (fishbone)
- Check Sheet
- Contingency Planning (PDPC)
- Control Chart
- Flowchart
- Force Field Diagram
- Gantt, PERT, and CPM Diagram

- Histogram
- Matrix Diagram
- Pareto Chart
- Prioritization Matrices
- Radar Chart
- Run Chart
- Scatter Diagram
- Stratification
- Tree Diagram

These tools and techniques are described in both *The Memory Jogger*™ and *The Memory Jogger Plus+*®.

While this list may appear daunting, teams should keep in mind that the best time for teams to learn these tools and techniques is when they are needed. This just-in-time training allows team members to retain the new information they have learned and to fully participate and contribute as they are learning about these tools and techniques.

16 Guidelines for Teams to Work Effectively

Generally, teams that are effective establish rules and guidelines for themselves, abide by the ones that work, and abolish the ones that don't.

These 16 guidelines are intended to help teams establish their own processes for working effectively as a team.

1. Establish clear goals and objectives that all team members accept. Members, in accepting the goals of the team, need to feel they have some ownership in achieving their goals. Team members need to be a part of developing the team's goals from the initial stages.

Objectives of the team must be clear, and at least in part, created by the members of the team. Members will be more willing to support what they have helped create. When the team creates its own goals, all the members will more likely be committed to accomplishing them than meeting goals created by others outside the team.

2. Let each team define its own standards of performance. Teams need to have their own standards, not standards that have been dictated to them. It is very important for members to have standards that they believe they can live by. Members must have the desire to achieve and believe that they can "make things happen." When teams define their own standards of performance, they help to ensure that members work as a team to assign tasks, set goals, timetables, deadlines for projects, and so forth.

3. Allow members to disagree as a constructive way to resolve problems and prevent long-term conflict within the team. It is important that members feel comfortable enough with each other to disagree. However, members need to recognize warning signs of conflict that may damage the team's effectiveness in the future. Healthy disagreement is good, and should be promoted, however, team leaders should be able to determine when healthy disagreement is heading toward conflict that may be detrimental to the team. When team leaders realize that relations are being strained, they should back up, explore areas of agreement, and bring the team back together on the same path.

An effective way to resolve conflict is to take a time out, and not to rush the process. Let all the members who have an opinion on the situation express themselves fully. Don't allow interruptions. This will encourage shy members to voice their opinions. Once the disagreement is on the table, team leaders may reflect on it, make certain that it is understood by the group, and then open a discussion. Make certain that every point is fully explored and work toward reaching an agreement. If, at a particular meeting, agreement cannot be reached, leave the issue as an item to be discussed at the next meeting.

4. Review past actions as a learning tool in planning tasks and projects for the future. Review what the team has done and let this information provide the learning for team members in future planning. This may help prevent the team from repeating earlier mistakes.

5. Make decisions by consensus with consideration of alternatives. Teams should review alternatives, discuss them fully, and address individual benefits and weaknesses. If a team member has an good alternative that is not fully discussed, it's possible the individual may be less of a participant in the future. If members feel their ideas are not given full consideration, and not getting the recognition they deserve, they tend to ease off in their participation. When teams consider alternatives fully, and then make decisions by consensus, all the members are involved and feel they have a part in the process. Consensus is reached when all the team members can live with a decision, but may not feel it is the *best* decision.

6. Remain cohesive and maintain a sense of unity. Group cohesiveness, which allows members to see themselves as parts of an integrated unit, is very important. Cohesiveness gives teams strength, a sense of purpose, and allows them to explore their potential for innovative ideas, creative solutions, and unencumbered productivity and effort.

7. Strive for synergy. Synergy is when the whole is greater than the sum of its parts. One person's idea may trigger another idea that builds on the first, and another idea that builds again on the previous idea, and another idea that again builds, until the idea is a creation grander than any single idea combined with another. People spin off other people's ideas, build on them, piggyback, and synergy results.

8. Develop a comfortable working atmosphere in which people are alert and fully involved. From when a meeting starts until the end, everyone needs to be involved. Effective leaders ensure this happens. Team members are not given the chance to lay back or remain uninvolved. Leaders may need to draw individuals into the meeting so they are full participants. A positive, active, psychological climate will generate more creativity.

9. Use physical space in a way that is conducive to the team process. People need the freedom to can get up and move, write on flip charts or use the overhead and put something on a transparency, write something on a board, or play a videotape.

10. Listen to each other and provide useful feedback. Listening is crucial. Listening should be taught and practiced by team leaders. Leaders can do a good job of role modeling by paraphrasing, reflecting, and using questioning techniques to ensure team members are really listening to each other. When team members listen to each other, they can provide useful feedback and concentrate on the team's synergy. If people don't feel that they are heard, they stop sharing their ideas with others.

11. Use constructive criticism to facilitate group interaction. Sometimes a particular point or approach to something may not be appropriate. If it is not appropriate, team leaders need to point this out. Personal criticisms should not be tolerated. Teams should focus their criticisms on acts or processes, not individuals. Leaders should provide feedback as soon as it is appropriate to do so. Once an issue has been dealt with, move on. It is important to immediately attempt to resolve potentially explosive situations. Occasionally, when someone plays the role of devil's advocate, it can be a constructive way to stimulate discussion. Used too often, this technique can lose its effectiveness.

12. Allow members to express their ideas fully and frankly. Intercept or minimize personal agendas. Personal agendas are always a problem when they exist. Personal agendas are actually a smokescreen that members create when they have a personal interest at stake in an idea, argument, task, project, or team, but they are attempting to mask their true motives. Personal agendas detract from the climate of trust. Eliminating or minimizing personal agendas is vital to improving team member interactions. Team members need to be informed of what is occurring. Honestly is always the best policy—candor between team members facilitates communication, and improves the team process.

13. Recognize individuals for the contributions they make within the team. Reinforcement and recognition can be a celebration of the team's accomplishments or the accomplishments of individual team members. Recognizing an individual may be as simple as noting the member's idea or action in the meeting minutes. Team leaders need to recognize individuals for the knowledge they bring to meetings and provide them with an incentive to continue sharing their ideas and commitment to the team.

14. Assist members when it ensures successful completion of team goals. At times, members may need "an assist." Teams can help these members by offering encouragement, or asking a question to help stimulate their thinking. Teams facilitate individuals, rather than expecting individuals to struggle alone in accomplishing their tasks.

15. Highly value creative approaches to problems, as unusual or impossible as they may sound initially. In some cases a creative approach can be branded as crazy. People can laugh at a creative approach. When people laugh at a new idea, team members may be reluctant to share their ideas if they are different. The most effective teams will put a real value on creative approaches to a problem.

16. Incorporate flexibility in the team's thoughts and actions. Rigidity and barriers stifle creativity. Asking teams to remain flexible requires a certain grace in allowing team members to decide how they will work together, accomplish their goals, and the methods they will use in producing results. Flexibility allows people to grow, feel free to make mistakes, and have faith in their ability to contribute to the team's achievements.

This page is intentionally left blank.

Exercise 3 Instructions

What are Some Qualities of Effective Teams?

Purpose

When organizations begin teams, there are certain qualities of team dynamics that the team leaders, sponsors, and participants will want to understand. It is important that everyone understands the possible dynamics and varied qualities of teams before the team begins to focus its improvement effort on a selected process. This exercise is designed to help team members develop a common understanding of team member relationships *and* reach consensus on their importance.

Preparation
- Give each participant a copy of the exercise.
- Provide enough pens and pencils for everyone.
- Lay out several multicolored felt tip markers for anyone to use.
- Set up a flip chart or writing board in the area.

Process
- Ask participants to read each statement in Exercise 2. Encourage them to complete the exercise by following their "gut" or initial response to each statement. Instruct participants to agree or disagree, or strongly agree or disagree with the statement, based on their perception of the dynamics of an effective team.
- Allow 5 minutes for participants to complete the exercise.
- Attempt to bring participants to consensus on each statement. If more participants disagree than agree with any statement, advise participants to review the statement(s) before they begin working to improve a process. Training on a specific team dynamic may be required as the team grows.

Discussion
- Work through the statements one by one, moving from 1 to 10.
- Attempt to reach consensus on each statement. Consensus means that each person can live with a decision, but may not feel it is the *best* decision.
- Close the discussion by identifying which behaviors and activities that, if developed more fully throughout the organization, can have the most positive effect on the culture of the organization.

- ▶ Time required: 60–75 minutes total
- ▶ Group size: Optimum is 4–9 people, but up to 20 people is acceptable

Consensus
Each person can live with a decision,
but may not feel it is the *best* decision.

Exercise 3
What are Some Qualities of Effective Teams?

Survey your team—not everyone will agree.

After you read the statement, agree or disagree, or strongly agree or disagree with the statement, based on your perception of the dynamics of an effective team.

1 An effective team establishes clear goals and objectives, which have been developed and accepted by the team.

   ❐ Strongly Disagree   ❐ Disagree   ❐ Agree   ❐ Strongly Agree

2 An effective team establishes standards of performance for itself, but its performance is measured by an outside source.

   ❐ Strongly Disagree   ❐ Disagree   ❐ Agree   ❐ Strongly Agree

3 An effective team considers all alternatives before making decisions. Decisions are made by consensus, not by vote.

   ❐ Strongly Disagree   ❐ Disagree   ❐ Agree   ❐ Strongly Agree

4 An effective team is flexible and allows most of its members to participate and influence decisions.

   ❐ Strongly Disagree   ❐ Disagree   ❐ Agree   ❐ Strongly Agree

5 An effective team is willing to give and accept feedback. All feedback is non-personal and is considered positive.

   ❐ Strongly Disagree   ❐ Disagree   ❐ Agree   ❐ Strongly Agree

6 An effective team achieves better results than any of its individuals working alone.

   ❐ Strongly Disagree   ❐ Disagree   ❐ Agree   ❐ Strongly Agree

7 An effective team welcomes quick agreement as an effective way to ensure that most aspects of a situation are addressed.

Exercise 3

❏ Strongly Disagree   ❏ Disagree   ❏ Agree   ❏ Strongly Agree

8 An effective team welcomes creative approaches to improving processes.

❏ Strongly Disagree   ❏ Disagree   ❏ Agree   ❏ Strongly Agree

9 An effective team uses the appropriate tool to supplement the team process.

❏ Strongly Disagree   ❏ Disagree   ❏ Agree   ❏ Strongly Agree

10 An effective team does not allow hidden agendas to interfere with the team process.

❏ Strongly Disagree   ❏ Disagree   ❏ Agree   ❏ Strongly Agree

NOTES

Chapter 4
Roles and Responsibilities in the Team Process

Key Points

- Roles people take in the team process
- Team members and their responsibilities to the team
- Some behaviors and learning styles common among team members

There are numerous roles and responsibilities in any successful team environment. Each member of the team should be aware of these roles and responsibilities and should actively display the characteristics associated with them. The knowledge of these roles and responsibilities directly influences the climate of the team.

The Types of Roles People Take in the Team Process

The primary roles associated with teams are:

Steering Committee. The steering committee is comprised of people in top management. This committee needs to lead the organization in its TQM and team efforts, including: 1) creating a vision and mission for the organization, 2) designing an implementation plan, 3) being the driving force for change, 4) creatively balancing the short-term needs with long-term goals that are focused on customer needs, 5) implementing the plan, 6) maintaining the plan through monitoring and periodic review, and 7) improvement of the process within the organization.

Manager and Supervisor. Middle management needs to: 1) develop the functional activities that meet the organization's vision and mission, 2) align the top executives' vision with the team's needs, 3) provide feedback to top executives based on the data developed by the teams, 4) coordinate team activities, offer advice on selecting issues, 5) provide needed resources, 6) remove barriers, 7) assist in implementing solutions, and 8) recognize team and team member achievements. Managers normally only participate on teams of managers. If they are involved with other teams, barriers are often raised unintentionally. In addition, the presence of management often makes teams feel that they are not really trusted to make decisions.

Sponsor. Team sponsors are individuals that empower a team. Sponsors are the primary conduit between the team and upper management. Sponsors must be able to 1) remove barriers, 2) ensure implementation, 3) follow up, 4) monitor, and 5) provide long-term support, rewards and recognition. Sponsors must also often function as coaches if the team requests it.

Facilitator. Facilitators often serve a critical role in the early stages of a team but are really striving to work themselves out of a job. Facilitators are present to: 1) bring out the opinions of the less vocal members of the team, 2) keep the team moving toward its objectives, 3) serve as process experts, and 4) provide stability to the team. Successful facilitators will provide assistance to the team leader by seeking everyone's opinions, being a resource of tools and techniques both for problem solving and team dynamics, summarize key points for the team, and continuously strive for group consensus. Facilitators are selected for their skill of observation, empathy toward team members, flexibility, ability to remain neutral in all situations, perceptivity of changing group dynamics and needs, and focus on the team process and desired outcomes.

Team Leader. Team leaders are either appointed by team sponsors or selected by the team. Team leaders: 1) conduct meetings, 2) are responsible for preparing meetings, including the agenda and physical space, 3) participate with other members in contributing ideas and making decisions, 4) represent the team to management, and 5) are the key interface with other teams and support resources. Team leaders are selected for their ability to listen to others and accept their ideas. In addition, team leaders are enthusiastic about the project, available and sensitive to others, and have the ability to focus on the team's goals.

Team Member. Team members are "experts" in the process that is being worked on. They are the people who are actually working in the process, own it, or are customers or suppliers of the process. Team members: 1) share their experience and knowledge, 2) identify areas for improvement, and 3) work with the other team members to standardize, improve, and document their processes. Team members should be willing to concentrate on evolving from individuals who base their decisions solely on intuition, feelings, metaphors, stories, and rules of thumb to an integrated group of people who work with facts and base their decisions on those facts.

Most teams have between four and nine active participants who are working on operations of which they have common knowledge and involvement. Some common types of teams include:

- **Problem Teams.** These teams have traditionally had names such as Project Action Teams, Problem Teams, and Hit Teams. They are formed to address one specific problem and are usually disbanded after the situation is resolved.
- **Ongoing Teams.** These teams have traditionally had names such as Quality Circles, Process Improvement Teams, and Kaizen Teams. They are formed to address process improvement potentials in a contiguous work area and meet on an ongoing basis.

- **Management Teams.** These teams have traditionally had names such as Steering Committee, Strategic Action Teams, and Strategic Planning Teams. They are usually formed to address and review high-level, strategic-planning issues and are ongoing teams.

Team Members and their Responsibilities to the Team

Listening is the most often neglected communication skill. In the team environment, listening is vital. While most people speak about 125 words per minute, they can understand the spoken word at a rate of about 250 words per minute, and they can think at a rate of about 600 words per minute. Team members will be more effective listeners if they follow the six guidelines listed below.

When you are listening to someone talk, remember to:

1. **Give your undivided attention.** Check your mental "baggage." Stop what you are doing and tune in to the speaker. Try to get into the speaker's channel of thoughts and ideas.
2. **Take responsibility for comprehending.** Do not take the attitude that it is the speaker's responsibility to pound ideas into your head. Make it your business to comprehend what's being said. Look for examples from your own experience to support or explain the speaker's thoughts. Rephrase the speakers ideas; put them into your own vocabulary.
3. **Listen to understand rather than to refute.** This does not exclude criticism of the speaker's thoughts; it does exclude such criticism before the speaker is finished. Analyze the speaker's ideas while the person is talking, but do not argue—the speaker may bring up a point later that may change your mind. Try to understand first and evaluate second.
4. **Control your emotions.** Listen for ideas to evaluate on their own merits—not on the opinion you hold of the person who states them. Try to identify words that are emotionally loaded, and recognize them for what they are; blocks to communication. React to the speaker's ideas, not the speaker's vocabulary, personal mannerisms, dress, or other qualities that may distract you from what the speaker is communicating.
5. **Listen for the main ideas, not the details.** Specific facts or individual statements may be interesting or sound important, but usually a speaker is offering them in support of an idea. If you zero in on one part, you may miss the whole.
6. **Put your mind to work.** Your mind can move much faster than a person can speak. People generally speak at 250 words per minute and think at about 600 words per minute. Use this "lag time" to review, repeat, forecast, summarize, and paraphrase the speaker's remarks. It will improve both your comprehension and retention.

Some Team Member Behaviors and Learning Styles

Individuals, as they work in teams, are likely to demonstrate a wide variety of different behaviors. Team members need to be ready and able to work out the issues around certain behaviors that can be destructive to teams. One method of dealing with these behaviors is to define and agree to a set of rules (ground rules) at the first team meeting. An effective method to accomplish this is to ask team members to list what they do not like about meetings they have attended or teams they have worked on, prioritize these issues, and then develop rules to deal with the most important issues. The types of behaviors that team members are likely to observe are:

- Someone who dominates the meeting or is highly argumentative
- Someone who is quiet, withdrawn, or doesn't want to be there
- Someone who digresses or loses focus
- Someone who acts as a know-it-all
- Someone who is stubborn
- Someone who gets stuck on a problem or issue

As team members discuss the types of behaviors they believe are acceptable within the team context, they will become more aware of their own behaviors. Some team members, at different times, may feel they are not contributing effectively to the team, perhaps because they can't get around a "personality flaw," or they don't know the contexts and ways in which adults best assimilate new information. It can be helpful for team members who wish to modify their own behaviors to be aware of how adults learn and use new information. For example:

- When adults receive information that conflicts with their accepted beliefs, they will integrate this information *more slowly than* when they receive information that matches their past actions.
- When adults learn new concepts, they understand them better if they are presented in more than one approach or context.
- Adults need to integrate new knowledge with knowledge gained previously.
- Adults need transition time and to focus their attention directly on integrating their new knowledge and skills.
- Adults prefer to learn new information with hands-on experience.

The benefits of growing teams to address processes are numerous. Having multiple input on a given process, involvement of the people closest to the process, clear identification of customer needs, and open channels of communication of all involved are just a few of the benefits.

This page is intentionally left blank.

Exercise 4 Instructions

How Can a Sponsor Help Your Team Grow?

Purpose

When people observe a team that is strong and functioning as a unit, the reason is probably that a sponsor made a significant investment of time and effort. Certain key behaviors and actions have been identified that can make a difference in the process of team growth. Participants will respond to the list of statements in this exercise based on how they view the behaviors and actions of a team sponsor.

Preparation

- ꙩ Give each participant a copy of the exercise.
- ꙩ Provide enough pens and pencils for everyone.
- ꙩ Lay out several multicolored felt tip markers for anyone to use.
- ꙩ Set up a flip chart or writing board in the area.

Process

- ꙩ Ask participants to carefully review the list of statements. Each one defines an action that is related to team growth. On the lefthand side of the statement, participants mark an "x" in one of the categories under the "Importance" column: extremely important, moderately important, limited importance, or not at all important. The placement of the "x" indicates how important it is to the participant that the team sponsor exhibits the behavior. On the righthand side of the statement, participants mark an "x" in one of the categories under the "Frequency" column: always, usually, sometimes, or never. The placement of the "x" indicates how frequently the participant observes the behavior in the team's sponsor.
- ꙩ Allow 5 minutes for participants to complete the exercise.
- ꙩ Ask participants to look at their evaluations for each statement in both the "Importance" and "Frequency" columns. Ask them to subtract the smaller number in one column from the larger number in the other column and record the difference in the gap category under the "Frequency" column.

Discussion

- ꙩ Ask participants to review their lists and identify the two or three biggest gaps. The key is to identify the statements rated as the most important that do not carry correspondingly high frequency ratings.
- ꙩ Ask participants to comment on at least one statement to the other members of the group that they feel is worthy of attention and improvement by the team.
- ꙩ After all the participants have had a chance to comment, review any statements that have not been covered and discuss their importance.

▶ Time required: 60–90 minutes total
▶ Group size: Optimum is 4–9 people, but up to 20 people is acceptable

Exercise 4
How Can A Sponsor Help Your Team Grow?

Time: 5 minutes

Survey your team members on the work values and skills they believe a sponsor should bring into action.

Part I: Carefully review the list of statements. Each one defines an action that is related to team growth. On the lefthand side of the statement, mark an "x" in one of the categories under the "Importance" column: extremely important, moderately important, limited importance, or not at all important. Where you place the "x" indicates how important you think it is that your team sponsor exhibits the behavior. On the righthand side of the statement, mark an "x" in one of the categories under the "Frequency" column: always, usually, sometimes, or never. Where you place the "x" indicates how frequently you observe the behavior in your team sponsor.

Part II: When your group has completed the exercise, you will be instructed to review your evaluations for each statement in both the "Importance" and "Frequency" columns. Subtract the smaller number in one column from the larger number in the other column and record the difference in the gap category under the "Frequency" column.

Importance   Frequency

My team's sponsor:

1 Knows the strengths of each member.
2 Takes time to listen attentively, and doesn't interrupt.
3 Makes communication a high priority.
4 Helps members to see how important they are to the team's overall success.
5 Provides clear direction ahead of time to minimize frustration
6 Assists the team in learning about specific problem-solving skills.
7 Provides recognition for accomplishments of the team and its members.
8 Gives team members an opportunity to share their knowledge with others.
9 Makes certain that upper-level management is aware of the team's progress.

9 4 1 0   9 4 1 0

45

Exercise 4

Importance		Frequency

Importance

Extremely Moderate Limited Not at All

☐☐☐☐ **10**   Follows through with team ideas to make sure   ☐☐☐☐☐
they are implemented.

☐☐☐☐ **11**   Says whether an idea can or cannot be used   ☐☐☐☐☐
and shares the reason with the team.

☐☐☐☐ **12**   Always communicates the belief: "None of us is as   ☐☐☐☐☐
smart as all of us."

9 4 1 0

Frequency

Always Usually Sometimes Never Gap

9 4 1 0

NOTES

NOTES

Exercise 5 Instructions

How Can a Facilitator Help Your Team Grow?

Purpose

When people observe a team that is strong and functioning as a unit, the reason is probably that a facilitator made a significant investment of time and effort. Certain key behaviors and actions have been identified that can make a difference in the process of team growth. Participants will respond to the list of statements in this exercise based on how they view the behaviors and actions of a facilitator.

Preparation

- Give each participant a copy of the exercise.
- Provide enough pens and pencils for everyone.
- Lay out several multicolored felt tip markers for anyone to use.
- Set up a flip chart or writing board in the area.

Process

- Ask participants to carefully review the list of statements. Each one defines an action that is related to team growth. On the lefthand side of the statement, participants mark an "x" in one of the categories under the "Importance" column: extremely important, moderately important, limited importance, or not at all important. The placement of the "x" indicates how important it is to the participant that the team facilitator exhibits the behavior. On the righthand side of the statement, participants mark an "x" in one of the categories under the "Frequency" column: always, usually, sometimes, or never. The placement of the "x" indicates how frequently the participant observes the behavior in the team's facilitator.
- Allow 5 minutes for participants to complete the exercise.
- Ask participants to look at their evaluations for each statement in both the "Importance" and "Frequency" columns. Ask them to subtract the smaller number in one column from the larger number in the other column and record the difference in the gap category under the "Frequency" column.

Discussion

- Ask participants to review their lists and identify the two or three biggest gaps. The key is to identify the statements rated as the most important that do not carry correspondingly high frequency ratings.
- Ask participants to comment on at least one statement to the other members of the group that they feel is worthy of attention and improvement by the team.
- After all the participants have had a chance to comment, review any statements that have not been covered and discuss their importance.

▶ Time required: 30–45 minutes total
▶ Group size: Optimum is 4–9 people, but up to 20 people is acceptable

Exercise 5
Time: 5 minutes

How Can A Facilitator Help Your Team Grow?
Survey your team members on the work values and skills they believe a facilitator should bring into action.

Part I: Carefully review the list of statements. Each one defines an action that is related to team growth. On the lefthand side of the statement, mark an "x" in one of the categories under the "Importance" column: extremely important, moderately important, limited importance, or not at all important. Where you place the "x" indicates how important you think it is that your team sponsor exhibits the behavior. On the righthand side of the statement, mark an "x" in one of the categories under the "Frequency" column: always, usually, sometimes, or never. Where you place the "x" indicates how frequently you observe the behavior in your team sponsor.

Part II: When your group has completed the exercise, you will be instructed to review your evaluations for each statement in both the "Importance" and "Frequency" columns. Subtract the smaller number in one column from the larger number in the other column and record the difference in the gap category under the "Frequency" column.

Importance

Frequency

Extremely / Moderate / Limited / Not at All		**My team's facilitator:**	Always / Usually / Sometimes / Never / Gap	
☐☐☐☐	**1**	Knows the strengths of each member.	☐☐☐☐☐	
☐☐☐☐	**2**	Takes time to listen attentively, and doesn't interrupt.	☐☐☐☐☐	
☐☐☐☐	**3**	Makes communication a high priority.	☐☐☐☐☐	
☐☐☐☐	**4**	Helps members to see how important they are to the team's overall success.	☐☐☐☐☐	
☐☐☐☐	**5**	Provides clear direction ahead of time to minimize frustration.	☐☐☐☐☐	
☐☐☐☐	**6**	Assists the team in learning about specific problem-solving skills.	☐☐☐☐☐	
☐☐☐☐	**7**	Provides recognition for accomplishments of the team and its members.	☐☐☐☐☐	
☐☐☐☐	**8**	Gives team members an opportunity to share their knowledge with others.	☐☐☐☐☐	
☐☐☐☐	**9**	Makes certain that upper-level management is aware of the team's progress.	☐☐☐☐☐	

9 4 1 0

9 4 1 0

Exercise 5

Importance   Frequency

| Extremely | Moderate | Limited | Not at All | | | Always | Usually | Sometimes | Never | Gap |

☐☐☐☐ **10**   Follows through with team ideas to make sure they are implemented.   ☐☐☐☐☐

☐☐☐☐ **11**   Says whether an idea can or cannot be used and shares the reason with the team.   ☐☐☐☐☐

☐☐☐☐ **12**   Always communicates the belief: "None of us is as smart as all of us."   ☐☐☐☐☐
9 4 1 0   9 4 1 0

NOTES

NOTES

Exercise 6 Instructions

How Can A Leader Help Your Team Grow?

Purpose

When people observe a team that is strong and functioning as a unit, the reason is probably that a leader made a significant investment of time and effort. Certain key behaviors and actions have been identified that can make a difference in the process of team growth. Participants will respond to the list of statements in this exercise based on how they view the behaviors and actions of a team leader.

Preparation

- Give each participant a copy of the exercise.
- Provide enough pens and pencils for everyone.
- Lay out several multicolored felt tip markers for anyone to use.
- Set up a flip chart or writing board in the area.

Process

- Ask participants to carefully review the list of statements. Each one defines an action that is related to team growth. On the lefthand side of the statement, participants mark an "x" in one of the categories under the "Importance" column: extremely important, moderately important, limited importance, or not at all important. The placement of the "x" indicates how important it is to the participant that the team leader exhibits the behavior. On the righthand side of the statement, participants mark an "x" in one of the categories under the "Frequency" column: always, usually, sometimes, or never. The placement of the "x" indicates how frequently the participant observes the behavior in the team's leader.
- Allow 5 minutes for participants to complete the exercise.
- Ask participants to look at their evaluations for each statement in both the "Importance" and "Frequency" columns. Ask them to subtract the smaller number in one column from the larger number in the other column and record the difference in the gap category under the "Frequency" column.

Discussion

- Ask participants to review their lists and identify the two or three biggest gaps. The key is to identify the statements rated as the most important that do not carry correspondingly high frequency ratings.
- Ask participants to comment on at least one statement to the other members of the group that they feel is worthy of attention and improvement by the team.
- After all the participants have had a chance to comment, review any statements that have not been covered and discuss their importance.

▶ Time required: 60–90 minutes total
▶ Group size: Optimum is 4–9 people, but up to 20 people is acceptable

Exercise 6
How Can A Leader Help Your Team Grow?

Time: 5 minutes

Survey your team members on the work values and skills they believe a leader should bring into action.

Part I: Carefully review the list of statements. Each one defines an action that is related to team growth. On the lefthand side of the statement, mark an "x" in one of the categories under the "Importance" column: extremely important, moderately important, limited importance, or not at all important. Where you place the "x" indicates how important you think it is that your team leader exhibits the behavior. On the righthand side of the statement, mark an "x" in one of the categories under the "Frequency" column: always, usually, sometimes, or never. Where you place the "x" indicates how frequently you observe the behavior in your team leader.

Part II: When your group has completed the exercise, you will be instructed to review your evaluations for each statement in both the "Importance" and "Frequency" columns. Subtract the smaller number in one column from the larger number in the other column and record the difference in the gap category under the "Frequency" column.

Importance   Frequency

Extremely	Moderate	Limited	Not at All		**My team's leader:**	Always	Usually	Sometimes	Never	Gap
☐	☐	☐	☐	**1**	Knows the strengths of each member.	☐	☐	☐	☐	☐
☐	☐	☐	☐	**2**	Takes time to listen attentively, and doesn't interrupt.	☐	☐	☐	☐	☐
☐	☐	☐	☐	**3**	Makes communication a high priority.	☐	☐	☐	☐	☐
☐	☐	☐	☐	**4**	Helps members to see how important they are to the team's overall success.	☐	☐	☐	☐	☐
☐	☐	☐	☐	**5**	Provides clear direction ahead of time to minimize frustration.	☐	☐	☐	☐	☐
☐	☐	☐	☐	**6**	Assists the team in learning about specific problem-solving skills.	☐	☐	☐	☐	☐
☐	☐	☐	☐	**7**	Provides recognition for accomplishments of the team and its members.	☐	☐	☐	☐	☐
☐	☐	☐	☐	**8**	Gives team members an opportunity to share their knowledge with others.	☐	☐	☐	☐	☐
☐	☐	☐	☐	**9**	Makes certain that upper-level management is aware of the team's progress.	☐	☐	☐	☐	☐

9 4 1 0   9 4 1 0

Exercise 6

Importance   Frequency

Extremely	Moderate	Limited	Not at All			Always	Usually	Sometimes	Never	Gap

☐☐☐☐ **10** Follows through with team ideas to make sure   ☐☐☐☐☐
they are implemented.

☐☐☐☐ **11** Says whether an idea can or cannot be used and   ☐☐☐☐☐
shares the reason with the team.

☐☐☐☐ **12** Always communicates the belief: "None of us is   ☐☐☐☐☐
9 4 1 0   as smart as all of us."   9 4 1 0

NOTES

NOTES

Exercise 7 Instructions

How Can Each Member Help the Team Grow?

Purpose

When people observe a team that is strong and functioning as a unit, the reason is probably that all the team members made a significant investment of time and effort. Certain key behaviors and actions have been identified that can make a difference in the process of team growth. Review the following list of twelve statements carefully.

Preparation
- Give each participant a copy of the exercise.
- Provide enough pens and pencils for everyone.
- Lay out several multicolored felt tip markers for anyone to use.
- Set up a flip chart or writing board in the area.

Process
- Ask participants to carefully review the list of statements. Each one defines an action that is related to team growth. On the lefthand side of the statement, participants mark an "x" in one of the categories under the "Importance" column: extremely important, moderately important, limited importance, or not at all important. The placement of the "x" indicates how important it is to the participant that the other team members exhibit the behavior. On the righthand side of the statement, participants mark an "x" in one of the categories under the "Frequency" column: always, usually, sometimes, or never. The placement of the "x" indicates how frequently the participant observes the behavior in the team's other members.
- Allow 5 minutes for participants to complete the exercise.
- Ask participants to look at their evaluations for each statement in both the "Importance" and "Frequency" columns. Ask them to subtract the smaller number in one column from the larger number in the other column and record the difference in the gap category under the "Frequency" column.

Discussion
- Ask participants to review their lists and identify the two or three biggest gaps. The key is to identify the statements rated as the most important that do not carry correspondingly high frequency ratings.
- Ask participants to comment on at least one statement to the other members of the group that they feel is worthy of attention and improvement by the team.
- After all the participants have had a chance to comment, review any statements that have not been covered and discuss their importance.

▶ Time required: 60–90 minutes total
▶ Group size: Optimum is 4–9 people, but up to 20 people is acceptable

Exercise 7
Time: 5 minutes

How Can Each Member Help the Team Grow?

Survey your team members on the work values and skills they believe they should bring into action.

Part I: Carefully review the list of statements. Each one defines an action that is related to team growth. On the lefthand side of the statement, mark an "x" in one of the categories under the "Importance" column: extremely important, moderately important, limited importance, or not at all important. Where you place the "x" indicates how important you think it is that the other team members exhibit the behavior. On the righthand side of the statement, mark an "x" in one of the categories under the "Frequency" column: always, usually, sometimes, or never. Where you place the "x" indicates how frequently you observe the behavior in other team members.

Part II: When your group has completed the exercise, you will be instructed to review your evaluations for each statement in both the "Importance" and "Frequency" columns. Subtract the smaller number in one column from the larger number in the other column and record the difference in the gap category under the "Frequency" column.

Importance   Frequency

Extremely / Moderate / Limited / Not at All		My team's members:	Always / Usually / Sometimes / Never / Gap
☐☐☐☐	**1**	Know each other's strengths.	☐☐☐☐☐
☐☐☐☐	**2**	Take time to listen attentively, and don't interrupt.	☐☐☐☐☐
☐☐☐☐	**3**	Make communication a high priority.	☐☐☐☐☐
☐☐☐☐	**4**	Help other members to see how important they are to the team's overall success.	☐☐☐☐☐
☐☐☐☐	**5**	Provide clear direction ahead of time to minimize frustration.	☐☐☐☐☐
☐☐☐☐	**6**	Assist other team members in learning about specific problem-solving skills.	☐☐☐☐☐
☐☐☐☐	**7**	Recognize individual and team accomplishments.	☐☐☐☐☐
☐☐☐☐	**8**	Give other team members an opportunity to share their knowledge.	☐☐☐☐☐
☐☐☐☐	**9**	Make certain that upper-level management is aware of the team's progress.	☐☐☐☐☐

9 4 1 0   9 4 1 0

57

Exercise 7

Importance   Frequency

| Extremely | Moderate | Limited | Not at All | | | Always | Usually | Sometimes | Never | Gap |

☐☐☐☐ **10** Follow through with team ideas to make sure they are implemented.   ☐☐☐☐☐

☐☐☐☐ **11** Say whether an idea can or cannot be used and share the reason with the team.   ☐☐☐☐☐

☐☐☐☐ **12** Always communicate the belief: "None of us is as smart as all of us."   ☐☐☐☐☐

9 4 1 0   9 4 1 0

NOTES

Chapter 5
Growing Teams

Key Points

- Resistance to change: what can management expect?
- Six actions for management when teaming efforts are resisted
- A process model to help teams track their process

The philosophy of management still alive today is that people are hired to work and not to think. The message has been "We pay you to do a job and we don't want your ideas on how to do it." This philosophy was developed at a time when most workers were uneducated and received their instruction on what to do and how to do it from their managers. In the last century, employee education levels have increased significantly. Today there is a growing recognition that employees know more about their job functions than their managers. Teamwork is a key part of the cultural change that must occur for this knowledge to transcend the traditional Taylor philosophy. (Taylor's philosophy is briefly explained in the introduction.)

Resistance to Change: What's Management to Do?

Teaming is a conceptually simple process but difficult to implement. Teaming to most individuals in an organization is foreign. Teams may be together for short periods of time or for as many as two or three years, depending on the project or purpose of the team. People often are on more than one team at any given time. As an organization begins to ask people to participate on teams, some typical concerns pop into employees' minds:

- Why do they want us to work in groups? We get paid as individuals.
- Is this another management trick to get us to work harder?

There are always some people in organizations who will be skeptical of any change, which can create resistance and conflict throughout the organization. It is the job of managers, supervisors, facilitators, and trainers to help employees feel comfortable with the transition to teaming.

Once managers answer the question of why they are supporting teams, they may initially encounter employees who feel uncomfortable in a new routine. "My boss always told me what to do, now he is asking my opinion and recording it on a flip chart."

Employees may feel that the process of teaming is "being done" to them and not by them. To help employees feel less threatened, managers should provide broad guidelines for a team's actions, and give the team members the freedom to choose how they should conduct themselves within these guidelines.

This uncomfortable or awkward feeling is natural and leaders or facilitators need to make sure that all members understand the process, their roles and responsibilities. The person who knows the most about a process is the one who is working within it. (Or *around* it, if the process isn't a good one.) No matter how the process was originally designed, the individual currently performing the function understands the minute details of the current process best.

In the "old way" of doing things, this process expert had little impact or ability to influence how the process was performed. As organizations continue to focus on continuous improvement, the process experts must be involved in maximizing the functions they are performing. If organizations fail to use teams and involve the process experts, they will continue to lose these improvement opportunities. This team approach needs to function at every level of the organization and in every process. This focus on processes must clearly define the needs of the customer before organizations invest in gathering the resources to improve the processes. If organizations fail to do this, they will fall into the trap of merely starting teams, not *growing* them. Organizations that start teams often waste large amounts of resources improving processes that should not exist. It is more important to put the time, resources, and effort into doing the right things right than to doing everything right or random things right.

Fear of the unknown often arises as teams begin to move forward. Teams may ask "What do we do next?" Appropriate training, a problem-solving methodology (see Chapter 8), frequent and clear communication from management and team leaders about expectations, and adequate resource support are ways to reduce fear.

Some team members or team leaders may feel that they are losing their empire. "I've been in the department for 15 years and worked my way up to a lead position and now the team is taking over my job!" A very real reaction.

"Have I been doing my job wrong all these years?" Managers should recognize this question as self-doubt or diminished self-esteem. "I have lost face with my fellow workers. I have failed." Past practices got you through to the next day, month, or year. However, organizations need to assure their employees that their organizations are evolving, not simply surviving. "We need new approaches for our future direction." "Join the effort and put the same energy into the future as you have in the past." "We want you on the team since you are a valuable resource."

These are the messages to communicate clearly and frequently.

Other setbacks or mindsets that may prompt employees to resist the initial effort to grow teams are:

- Management announces that the schedule is set, then says nothing for three months.
- People make an initial commitment, but don't follow through.
- People won't make a commitment because they believe teaming will give them more work.
- Supervisors won't allow anyone in their department to attend team meetings.

When People Resist Teaming Efforts: Six Actions that Can Help

When organizations start to grow teams, management should be savvy enough to expect resistance and plan how to work with it. One simple, conceptual way to work with resistance is to ask everyone to believe the organization's future depends on a culture change—from belief comes the commitment and actions to make change happen. A more formal structure for dealing with resistance is to consistently apply the following six actions in forming teams:

Action 1
Hand pick team members. This process should be a combination of team sponsors and team leaders nominating individuals, as well as interested individuals volunteering for the team. If possible, the exact number of team members needed should be solicited. A well-functioning team usually has no fewer that four members and no more than nine. This range of the number of people on a team will encourage a diversity of good ideas without overwhelming the team with too many ideas, which can bring teams to inaction. In determining who the best candidates are for the team, sponsors and team leaders should discuss among themselves: "Why is this the right person for the team? Does this person have an interest in the process, knowledge of it, and does this person share a similar philosophy of our communication methodologies?" If more than the required number of team members has been solicited, team leaders and sponsors should be sensitive to the feelings of the volunteers who have not been chosen for the team. These volunteers should be included in some fashion in the team process. They can be asked to serve as advisors or participate on another team that is working on a different aspect of the process.

Action 2
Offer team-building training. Team members should be trained in basic teaming concepts, so they can experience the positive results that team building can accomplish. There are many good team-building tools and exercises, some of which appear in this book. Another good source is McBerr and Company. Some of the team-building exercises they offer are "The Caribbean," "Desert Survival," and "The Stuck Truck." Many human resource departments also offer this type of training. This type of training can be valuable when people feel strongly that the individual way is the best way. When they are exposed to the power of a team solu-

tion, they can be surprised in a very positive way.

Another valuable tool for improving teamwork is to ask team members to complete a personality profile. These profiles have no wrong answers, they are designed to facilitate an individual's understanding of other people's viewpoints and styles of interaction. Two of the most common personality profiles are the Herrmann Brain Dominance Profile and the Meyers-Briggs Type Indicator. (See Appendix A for more information.) When team members, leaders, and sponsors have this type of information, it can enhance the cooperation between team members.

Action 3
Work at developing team trust, confidence and camaraderie. Teams need to develop confidence in the team process and management's support of the process before they can really make it grow for them. If management tries to shortcut this growing process and immediately throws teams into working on problems without training, many of the team members will conclude that nothing has changed. Team members will feel that the team process is a waste of time rather than a value-added methodology.

Trust is enormously important. Without it, team members will never fully express their ideas. People don't want to appear stupid, be laughed at, or suggest ideas that may fail. Trust is built over a period of time, after solid footing is provided by management.

Action 4
Provide training on team tools. Using tools can help to facilitate the team process. The tools most frequently used are problem-solving tools, statistical methods, and planning tools. Many of these tools are designed to eliminate the fear of contribution or failure in a team process. Some of the other tools are designed to gather and display data that allow more informed decision making, or they allow teams to manipulate ideas in such a way as to expedite informed decision making and process-improvement planning.

Action 5
Establish team ground rules and measures. It is important that the team itself establish and follow a set of ground rules. Without ground rules it is very easy for teams to lose direction and long-term focus. Teams need to establish their criteria for success and how the criteria will be measured. These three elements—ground rules, criteria for success, and how to measure the criteria—enable teams to establish and maintain order, direction and focus. In addition, teams should establish measures of success for how well the team is performing in the team process. These measures should be evaluated after every team meeting.

Action 6
Work on an issue. At this point, teams should begin to work on the process that has been defined. Team members should keep in mind that their approach should follow the Plan, Do, Check, Act cycle.

Initial team projects should be kept short. If the proposed project can be completed within two months, this is a good time frame for a new team. The completed project will provide a basis for the organization to continue to grow the team, and to grow other teams as well. If the proposed project will take significantly longer than two months to complete, it should be reconsidered for another team or another time. It is difficult for team members, who are new to the team concept, to learn new tools, techniques, and methodologies *and* maintain a long-term focus on the project.

A Process Model to Help Teams Track Their Progress

A good process model that allows teams to track their progress is as follows:

Step 1
Agree on a purpose hierarchy. Team members should brainstorm a list of potential objectives for their team to accomplish. After brainstorming, the team should focus on fitting each objective into a hierarchy. This step will enable team members to focus on their customers, give them an initial visual image of what they want to accomplish, and understand what they may need to change to accomplish their objectives. By developing a purpose hierarchy, team members will focus on what their objectives need to be capable of in the future, not what is wrong with their process presently. This step is not intended to create a mission or vision, since neither one necessarily affects the organization's success.

Step 2
Develop a set of strategies that will help the team accomplish the selected objectives. These strategies should be under the control of the team, have a stated objective, and a description of what the new process will look like when it is implemented.

Step 3
Establish criteria for success and agree on how the criteria will be measured. The criteria for success should be established in conjunction with the needs of all the customers of the process. At least one measurement should be developed for each criteria. This is a step that is often overlooked.

Step 4
Propose action plans that will help the team accomplish their objectives. Just as in critical process development, this step ensures both horizontal and vertical linking of the team's activities and this ensures that the purpose is accomplished and that from the start, waste is not built into the system. In addition, these linked plans enable proper budgeting and team sponsors to remove barriers at a much earlier stage of the process. This step enables team members to prioritize actions and allows a comprehensive focus on the overall goal. A well-defined action plan enables concise measurement and tracking to be performed with a minimum of effort.

A good action plan should include a **SMART** matrix. This matrix captures the **Specific** to be accomplished, the **Measurable**, which will show it is accomplished, the **Assignment**, or who is responsible for its accomplishment, the **Resources** required to accomplish the Specific, and the **Time** to accomplish it. Creating the **SMART** matrix enables team members to participate and accept responsibility for the specifics they are best qualified to carry out.

Step 5
Set up a regularly scheduled review process. This process should have a standard format and be based on data. Finger pointing should be avoided. The review should focus on both the process and the results. Periodic reviews should be scheduled at least quarterly and the outcomes should be publicized. At the very least, the reviews should cover the specific activities that were planned, and what has been accomplished. The reviews should also consider the implications of the other information contained in the **SMART** matrix.

This page is intentionally left blank.

Exercise 8 Instructions

How Do the Members of Your Team Participate on the Team?

Purpose

As a leader or supervisor participates in the early growth of a team, it is vital to monitor the occurrence of the key factors that are commonly present in effective, developing teams. These factors include team member communication, behavior, and activity. In this exercise, participants review 10 key factors and circle the number on the scale that most accurately describes their team.

Preparation

- Give each participant a copy of the exercise.
- Provide enough pens and pencils for everyone.
- Lay out several multicolored felt tip markers for anyone to use.
- Set up a flip chart or writing board in the area.

Process

- Ask participants to read the 10 key factors of effective teams listed in Exercise 8. Encourage them to complete the exercise by following their "gut" or initial response to each statement. Instruct participants to circle the number that they believe best describes their team. A "1" is the lowest rating and indicates that many problems exist. A "5" is the highest rating and indicates that the team is strong and effective.
- Allow 4 minutes for participants to complete the exercise.

Discussion

- Work through the list in numerical order.
- Ask participants to call out the rating they selected for each item. The leader records the numbers on a pad or board. If desired, all numbers can be added and divided by the number of participants to get an overall rating.
- Provide participants with the opportunity to briefly discuss each item so they may develop a common agreement on why it is important. Also discuss what participants can do to improve the ratings if the exercise is done again in three months.

▶ Time required: 60–75 minutes total
▶ Group size: Optimum is 4–9 people, but up to 20 people is acceptable

Exercise 8
Time: 4 minutes

How Do the Members of Your Team Participate on the Team?

Poll your team members—you may get some surprising differences of opinion.

Review the 10 key factors of effective teams listed below. Draw a circle around the number that most accurately describes your team. A "1" is the lowest rating and indicates that many problems exist. A "5" is the highest rating and indicates that the team is strong and effective.

1 Purpose and objectives

1	2	3	4	5
Not clear and not understood by everyone				Clearly understood by everyone

2 Involvement/Participation

1	2	3	4	5
Some members are silent and contribute very little				All members are encouraged to participate

3 Conflict

1	2	3	4	5
Occurs continuously and is not dealt with properly				When it occurs, it is dealt with openly

4 Communication/Listening

1	2	3	4	5
Guarded: feelings are not freely expressed				Members feel free to say what is on their minds

Exercise 8

5 Leadership

1	2	3	4	5
Team leader plays a strong dominant role				Members share leadership role

6 Problem Solving

1	2	3	4	5
Tools have not been identified and agreed on for this purpose				Team members share knowledge of the tools

7 Meeting Climate

1	2	3	4	5
Formal, rigid, with many signs of tension				Members are relaxed and think meetings are fun

8 Roles and Assignments

1	2	3	4	5
Assignments are vague and not distributed evenly				Assignments are clear and involve all members

9 Creativity

1	2	3	4	5
No premium for "wild" ideas: they are in fact discouraged				Members use brainstorming often to seek fresh approaches

Exercise 8

10 *Self-Assessment*

1	2	3	4	5
There is never enough time for the team to evaluate its effectiveness				Team members frequently assess their progress

NOTES

Chapter 6
Nurturing Teams

Key Points

- Facets of empowerment
- Team growth: how can it be measured?
- Solicit feedback: try the customer-supplier map

Nurturing teams takes place at all levels of the organization. It begins at the highest levels of the organization and encompasses all aspects of the organization. It is not enough that management encourage people to work in teams. Management can truly empower employees, and thus nurture teams, by asking people to get involved in the team process, allow teams to make changes and improvements to their processes, give teams permission to choose the areas they want to improve, give its support by publicly recognizing team accomplishments or defending team failures, establish parameters for team projects, and share the responsibility of success and failure with team members.

Facets of Empowerment

Getting involved. "Get involved" can too easily be coined as a "catch phrase" and used superficially. Organizations who are redefining their cultural values should strive to involve the people who are "experts" at their jobs, not just managers. Involvement begins at the top and is expanded to the people who not only wish to participate, but who can offer their knowledge and skills in helping to improve a process or resolve a problem.

Power to make decisions. Management's power, strangely enough, lies partly in its ability to allow teams to make some decisions on their own. Having permission from management to make decisions is at the heart of team strength. Teams that are given the decision-making power to make and monitor changes to a process to improve it are empowered to produce effective solutions. Teams also need permission to work on processes that are not "broken," if they see a need for improvement. Too often organizations form teams and give them no power to prescribe changes or make small decisions that will help them move forward. Unfortunately, the nominal charter for many teams is to find the problem and give management a recommendation to fix it. This attitude and method does more to inhibit teamwork than it does to nurture it. This is just another manifestation of business as usual, rather than a true beginning of change in the culture of an organization.

Permission. Teams, to work effectively, need permission from management to make decisions that identify a specific process and to make improvements. Teams need clear communication from management that it is within their power to decide what to address and how to address it. Teams need to feel that they will not be second-guessed by management, they will have the flexibility, if necessary, to work outside the boundaries of how projects are normally handled, and to have permission to address "sacred cows."

Protection. Management offers protection to teams in the form of support: management publicly recognizes the achievements of individual members and the team as a whole, and management allows teams the freedom to fail. Teams can concentrate on identifying problems, generating ideas, and implementing and monitoring process improvements rather than feeling they are process "police" and have been asked to assign, assess, or establish blame. Managers can only empower teams to work on a process that is within each manager's span of control. If a manager does not own the process, the process owner must be involved from the beginning of the team process and continue to nurture the team as time goes on.

Parameters. Parameters are essential for nurturing teams. Parameters are the boundaries that management asks teams to operate within or that the solution must entail. This aspect of nurturing teams is often overlooked. Parameters are not to be construed as a solution, instead, they are useful to teams as guidelines to ensure the improvement process is meeting the needs of the organization. Parameters can be used to exclude certain solutions, but more importantly, to give teams a framework to work within as they develop solutions. Parameters allow teams to develop effective goals, measurements, and guidelines to be used in the improvement process. Parameters often include costs, time, staffing, and so on.

It is good to set parameters, but there guidelines for setting parameters that will separate workable goals from "doomed-from-the-start" goals. Follow these guidelines in creating goals for your team:

- Make sure each goal is realistic (perhaps get feedback from outside the team)
- Negotiate each goal and measurements of success
- Set up a timeline for completing each goal
- Write down the goals that team members have agreed to work toward, and how the team will measure each goal, then distribute the information to team members and appropriate managers
- Review and update the progress toward each goal on a regular basis
- Ensure adequate recognition for accomplishments
- Ensure timely, appropriate feedback

Measurements for accomplishing established goals should be doable, have a perceived value, and fall within the context of the process.

Teams, from the onset, should establish guidelines for their team process by first discussing issues concerning:

- Roles of team members
- Responsibilities of team members
- Process format that the team will follow
- Control measures
- Trust and conflict resolution
- Decision-making processes
- Team process evaluations
- Communication methodologies

Shared Responsibility. All of the members of a team need to take responsibility for their actions. They need to be willing to participate and complete the action items they agree to accomplish. Along with the power, permission and protection that teams ideally receive from management comes a shared responsibility for team members to work together and with management to accomplish their goals.

Team Growth: How Can It Be Measured?

Nurturing teams takes time, care, and dedication. One way to identify whether an organization attempts to nurture its teams or control them is to ask what criteria it sets for the progress of culture change within the organization. Does the organization measure the number of teams that have been established? The number of people involved in teams? Or does the organization celebrate the accomplishments of its process-focused teams and share the knowledge of how the team culture has an impact on its customers?

Teams should capitalize on internal feedback from all sources. If a team is in one area of the organization, it should solicit feedback from all other areas of the organization in which the process is active. People need to know how well their team is performing, how their team is helping to improve processes, and the strengths and weaknesses of their team. With feedback, the team can grow and get stronger.

There are frequent opportunities for getting feedback, however, these opportunities are often ignored. Teams need to take a proactive approach in getting feedback. If the feedback is from a customer of a process, it is invaluable. If it is from another source, it is still important. Meaningful feedback is one of the most powerful factors that contribute to team growth, nurturance, and development.

Teams should incorporate a method for soliciting feedback on their improvement processes. This can include surveys or questionnaires, interviews, inviting guests to attend team meetings, internally-developed data collected from direct customer contact, or other methods of opening lines of communication between teams and their customers. An effective tool to help teams set up a feedback process is the customer-supplier map. More complete information on the customer-supplier map is available in Chapter 3 of *Daily Management: A System for Individual and Organizational Optimization.*

This page is intentionally left blank.

Exercise 9 Instructions

How Effective is Your Team in Setting Goals?

Purpose
This exercise focuses participants on 16 essential attributes of workable goals, and asks them to evaluate their importance and occurance within the team environment. Setting workable goals is a key component in the long-term success of teams.

Preparation
- ⊃ Give each participant a copy of the exercise.
- ⊃ Provide enough pens and pencils for everyone.
- ⊃ Lay out several multicolored felt tip markers for anyone to use.
- ⊃ Set up a flip chart or writing board in the area.

Process
- ⊃ Ask participants to read the list of attributes in Exercise 9. Participants should check off three attributes of goal setting that are most important to them, and also three attributes that they feel are most lacking in their team's current goal-setting process. There are two columns, "Important," and "Lacking" set up for both evaluations.
- ⊃ Ask participants to form into groups, with four people to a group, and then to accomplish the following:
  1) For each attribute identified, state a reason either why it is important or why it may be lacking.
  2) Develop a list, by consensus, of the three most important attributes and the reasons why. (It's a good idea to limit one attribute to one sheet on the flip chart pad.)
  3) Develop a list, by consensus, of the three attributes most lacking in the current goal-setting process and the reasons why. (Again, limit one attribute to one sheet on the flip chart pad.)
- ⊃ Allow participants between 20 and 30 minutes to complete the exercise.

Discussion
- ⊃ With all the participants, review each team's results and integrate the lists and reasons. A few attributes will be common among the most important and most lacking. This commonality can be used to focus the participants on a few critical attributes.

- ▶ Time required: 60–75 minutes total
- ▶ Group size: Optimum is 4–9 people, but up to 20 people is acceptable

Consensus
Each person can live with a decision,
but may not feel it is the *best* decision.

Exercise 9

Time: 20–30 minutes

How Effective is Your Team in Setting Goals?

Complete this checklist and understand how your team members perceive the team's level of success.

Part I: Check off three attributes of goal setting that are most important to you, and also three attributes that you feel are most lacking in your team's current goal-setting process.

Part II: When you have joined a group, help to accomplish the following:
1) For each attribute identified, state a reason either why it is important or why it may be lacking in your team's goal-setting process.
2) Develop a list, by consensus, of the three most important attributes of setting goals and the reasons why they are important. (It's a good idea to limit one attribute to one sheet on the flip chart pad.)
3) Develop a list, by consensus, of the three attributes most lacking in your team's current goal-setting process and the reasons why you think they are lacking. (Again, limit one attribute to one sheet on the flip chart pad.)

		Important	Lacking	Reason(s)
1	Everyone participates	❑	❑	_____
2	Goals are clearly stated	❑	❑	_____
3	Timeline for completing goals	❑	❑	_____
4	Clear standards for measuring goals	❑	❑	_____
5	Goals are documented	❑	❑	_____
6	Compelling reason(s) for setting each goal	❑	❑	_____
7	Feedback on progress is timely	❑	❑	_____
8	Goals are realistic and attainable	❑	❑	_____
		Important	**Lacking**	**Reason(s)**

77

Exercise 9

9   Goals are reviewed and updated   ❑   ❑   _____

10   Team goals are compatible   ❑   ❑   _____
with company goals

11   Team members take respon-   ❑   ❑   _____
sibility for their actions

12   Benefits to completing goals   ❑   ❑   _____

13   Goals have parameters   ❑   ❑   _____

14   Goals are open to discussion   ❑   ❑   _____

15   Team members are empowered   ❑   ❑   _____
to set and accomplish goals

16   Recognition for accomplishing   ❑   ❑   _____
goals

NOTES

Chapter 7
Attitudes of a Team Builder

Key Points

- The power of a supportive team culture
- How attitudes affect the team culture
- How management can show it supports a team culture
- How team leaders, members, and facilitators can show they support a team culture
- "What's in it for me?" to support a team culture?

The most important aspect of growing teams is a positve attitude of the organization. The attitude and focus on teaming needs to start at the top. Managers must learn to give up the control that they have learned to exercise in favor of empowering employees to work in teams that have been formed around meeting the needs of customers.

Work with the Basics: Match Action to Attitude

Management often faces a dilemma in the early stages of using teams. It is often unwilling to allow teams to function on their own until they have demonstrated their ability to do so. However, teams cannot prove themselves until management allows them to do so. Therefore, team sponsors need to ensure the message teams receive is positive and reflects the following attitudes:

- **People must be communicated with openly and honestly and must be encouraged to communicate in the same fashion within the team.** Communication needs to be open, honest, encouraging, and requires a two-way effort. Feedback needs to be prompt, descriptive, and specific, however, it should not overload the person receiving the feedback. Before providing feedback, it is important to examine your own motives ad the person's readiness to receive the feedback.

- **Team members should be trained to do their jobs and to function as a team. Team members must understand what is to be done.** Team members should be adequately trained in their jobs, team concepts, and the use of problem-solving tools. The training needs to be in sufficient detail to allow application, not just conceptual knowledge. It is necessary for team members to have the ability to apply the right tool, methodology, or concept at the right time.

- **When people are selected to work on a team, they must have the technical competence, knowledge, and ability to work with others.** Characteristics to look for in each potential member are: good interpersonal skills, a willingness and ability to work with other people, an outward signal that indicates the person receives satisfaction from working with other people. Team members who have these characteristics improve a team's chance for success.

- **Expectations for the team must be realistic and specific.** Team members need to understand what is expected from them and perceive benefits of being on a team before they can completely embrace a project. With this information, the team can continuously improve and maintain a clear focus on the improvement and team process.

- **Team members must own the process being improved, whenever possible. Involve others outside the basic team that are also involved in the process.** A sense of ownership can be nurtured by having team members involved in goal setting, problem solving, and productivity improvement activities. People must feel a sense of ownership, truly be involved, as well as understand the benefits for themselves and their organization.

- **Resolve conflicts quickly to prevent them from becoming destructive.** Disagreement is a normal element of the team process, however, it should not get out of control. If disagreement grows into conflict, barriers may develop and impede the team's ability to function effectively. If conflicts are not resolved quickly, teams may become dysfunctional, lose their focus, and not achieve their goals.

- **Nurture trust and confidence. Teams should focus on this area and work closely with a sponsor.** Any agreements made with the team must be honored. Trust is absolutely crucial to the whole process of building teams.

- **Using positive feedback, reinforce observed team characteristics that facilitate teamwork and mutual support.** Team spirit can be encouraged by allowing people to work together and support each other on related activities.

- **Allow team members to get to know each other, and they will mutually respect one another's contributions.** It is important that team members take time to get to know and understand each other. When team members get to know the strengths and weaknesses of each other, the more open and effective their contributions become. Each team member has a tremendous hidden talent that needs to be uncovered and nurtured. A talent shared is one that can stimulate and energize a team.
- **Team members should regularly assess the team's growth against where**

they think it should be. The progress of the team process should be consistently measured.

Sponsors, team leaders, management, and steering committees should take every opportunity to increase the effectiveness of teams. This group has a wealth of experience that can directly influence team members' desires and abilities to function together.

How Management Can Show It Supports a Team Culture

Management can easily convey its support of the team culture in many ways. For example, people who have the role of sponsor, team leader, manager, or member of a steering committee, can follow a few simple guidelines:

- Listen and acknowledge ideas
- Praise team members as they learn
- Make team members think—reflect questions back to the team
- Allow team members to make mistakes and learn
- Share your experiences with a team only if members ask for input or direction
- Allow teams to come up with their own solutions
- Avoid making judgments
- Spend additional time with a team when necessary
- Be willing to personally train team members how to use specific tools or carry out specific procedures
- Focus on team concerns rather than your own
- Follow up on requests from a team
- Create positive team behavior through positive reinforcement
- Put other team members at ease by being at ease
- Do not point blame at team members

How Team Leaders, Members, and Facilitators Can Show They Support a Team Culture

Employees must take responsibility for their own destinies. They must realize that they can no longer blame management when something goes wrong. In an empowered organization, the employees are responsible for its success or failure. Attitudes of team members can be easily influenced by the actions they see from those above them, those who have participated on previous teams, and those participating on the same team. It is important that team members feel their contributions have value and that they are being heard. Team leaders and facilitators should be especially careful to elicit a response from each team member for each decision that is reached. Voting is not sufficient, consensus is required. If consensus is not reached, future decisions and actions by the team may become meaningless. No matter how often voting is done, or how strong the vote, it can never make a wrong right and it can never change the mind of an individual.

Some techniques that team leaders and facilitators can use to ensure team member participation include:

- When posing a question, pause for 10 seconds before selecting a respondent. Look around the group. Restate the question. Give everyone time to formulate a response. Then select a respondent.
- Ask some questions that everyone can respond to.
- When working on in-depth, thought-provoking issue, team members may want to take some individual quiet time to write down their responses.
- If the data is not available, ask team members to make an educated guess so the team can continue to work. When the meeting is over, find out the information that will validate or refute the guess.
- Complete a secret team evaluation after each meeting on the process checks that were agreed upon at the first meeting.
- Work in small subgroups when there are many issues to address.
- Develop a list of action items for each meeting and keep the list posted and updated.
- If there is major disagreement on individual steps, have individuals exchange roles. This will help the team members who disagree with one another to better understand other people's positions on an issue.
- Allow quiet time for team members to make decisions.

"What's in it for Me?" to Support a Team Culture?

To embark on the process of growing teams, organizations will need to commit to a change in management philosophy, establish an empowered culture, develop individual and team skills, remove traditional barriers within the organization, and dispel fear in team members. Teams must be motivated before they can change how they accomplish a process. Often this change requires learning and learning requires team members to take action. This action is frequently internal and they are free to act or not act in a specific manner. The most powerful motivator is an expected response to the "WIIFM" question. "WIIFM" is "What's in it for me?" If there is an insufficient answer to this question, the best intentions of management will be thwarted.

The "WIIFM" question is frequently addressed in the contracting process. A good contract with the team is a harbinger of success and directly affects the attitudes of both the team members and team sponsor. Measurable, attainable outcomes lead to a feeling of success that builds the strength of the team. Clear and open communication among team members and between a team and management also builds a healthy attitude toward the team process and achieving team goals.

Don't assume that team members will feel the team process is valuable in itself. Be ready to show them the value, keeping in mind that what is valuable for one person may not be valuable for another. It is the job of the team leader, facilitator, and management to show how a team will be useful. Be liberal with positive reinforcement: offer a pat on the back, encouragement, support for a job well done, and praise for small accomplishments. Don't wait for the end of a project to celebrate. Remember that teams need to know they are moving in the right direction. Be natural and sincere when you praise teams. Use the proposed outcome itself as a motivator. If teams are working on a project that is meaningful to them, improving a process can make their jobs easier.

Provide a positive climate for motivation. Even though motivation may be internally generated by some team members, not all of them will feel that way. Be prepared to stimulate their interest. A supportive attitude should be encouraged for and by each team member. A focus on shared problem-solving allows team members to cooperate and work together to solve problems, overcome barriers, and improve processes.

Teams may need a change of pace occasionally to maintain their interest in a project. A change of pace can be as simple as changing the time, location, or length of the meeting, bringing in lunch, or as complex as gathering new types of data, learning new tools, or practicing new presentation methodologies.

Positive organizational attitudes improve every team's chance of success and affect their ability to function effectively. Negative organizational attitudes are a recipe for failure. Teams must be grown and nurtured carefully or they will be perceived as "just another TQM program."

Exercise 10 Instructions

What Impact Does the Leader's Attitude Have on Growing Teams?

Purpose

When supervisors or group leaders have made a personal decision to support the growth of teams in the workplace, it becomes increasingly clear that their attitudes will have a significant impact. Participants will review a list of ten statements, which reflect a particular attitude that can affect team growth. Participants select three statements they would like to focus on to support team growth.

Preparation

- ○ Give each participant a copy of the exercise.
- ○ Provide enough pens and pencils for everyone.
- ○ Lay out several multicolored felt tip markers for anyone to use.
- ○ Set up a flip chart or writing board in the area.

Process

- ○ Ask participants to read the ten statements.
- ○ Instruct participants to select, in order of priority, (1 is top priority), the top three items that they think they should personally focus on to support team growth.
- ○ Allow participants five minutes to complete the exercise.
- ○ While participants are doing the exercise, the leader or facilitator draws a grid on the flip chart, with the numbers one through ten down the left side, and writes each participant's name across the top.

Discussion

- ○ Ask participants, one by one, to report on the statements they selected, and to identify the order of priority. As each person reports, write down the priority number in the appropriate column in the grid.
- ○ Explain that the benefit of this is to make the selection process visible, and since all statements are of value, "wrong" answers are not possible.
- ○ Review the list in order, asking the group to comment on what is important about each statement, especially statements that may not have been selected by anyone.

▶ Time required: 60–90 minutes
▶ Group size: Optimum is 4–9 people, but up to 20 people is acceptable

Time: 5 minutes

Exercise 10
What Impact Does the Leader's Attitude Have On Growing Teams?

Survey team leaders on which issues they believe they should focus on to support team growth.

The list that follows has ten statements, which reflect a particular attitude that can affect team growth. Which statements do you need to focus on to support team growth in your area? Prioritize the top three by putting the number in the box.
(1 is top priority.)

☐ **1** My goal is to talk with people openly and honestly and encourage them to do the same with me.

☐ **2** I provide employees with the required training to do their job and make sure they understand what is to be done.

☐ **3** When I hire people, I select those who have the required technical competence as well as the ability to work well with others.

☐ **4** Expectations that are realistic and specific will help people perform as a team.

☐ **5** Ownership is crucial to team building so I involve people in problem solving whenever possible.

☐ **6** While conflict in groups is normal, I work hard to resolve it quickly so it won't become destructive.

☐ **7** I work hard to develop trust and confidence in the process of growing a team.

☐ **8** When I see people working together, I provide positive feedback to reinforce their behavior.

☐ **9** I seek out ways to help team members get to know each other better, which helps them build respect for each other.

☐**10** I encourage the team to regularly assess its growth compared to where the team thinks it should be.

Exercise 11 Instructions

What Impact Does Each Member's Attitude Have on Growing Teams?

Purpose

When supervisors or group leaders have made a personal decision to support the growth of teams in the workplace, it becomes increasingly clear that their attitudes will have a significant impact. Participants will review a list of ten statements, which reflect a particular attitude that can affect team growth. Participants select three statements they would like to focus on to support team growth.

Preparation

- ○ Give each participant a copy of the exercise.
- ○ Provide enough pens and pencils for everyone.
- ○ Lay out several multicolored felt tip markers for anyone to use.
- ○ Set up a flip chart or writing board in the area.

Process

- ○ Ask participants to read the ten statements.
- ○ Instruct participants to select, in order of priority, (1 is top priority), the top three items that they think they should personally focus on to support team growth.
- ○ Allow participants five minutes to complete the exercise.
- ○ While participants are doing the exercise, the leader or facilitator draws a grid on the flip chart, with the numbers one through ten down the left side, and writes each participant's name across the top.

Discussion

- ○ Ask participants, one by one, to report on the statements they selected, and to identify the order of priority. As each person reports, write down the priority number in the appropriate column in the grid.
- ○ Explain that the benefit of this is to make the selection process visible, and since all statements are of value, "wrong" answers are not possible.
- ○ Review the list in order, asking the group to comment on what is important about each statement, especially statements that may not have been selected by anyone.

▶ Time required: 60–90 minutes total
▶ Group size: Optimum is 4–9 people, but up to 20 people is acceptable

Exercise 11
Time: 5 minutes

What Impact Does Each Member's Attitude Have On Growing Teams?

Survey your team members on which issues they believe they should focus on to support team growth.

The list that follows has ten statements, which reflect a particular attitude that can affect team growth. Which statements do you need to focus on to support team growth in your area? Prioritize the top three by putting the number in the box. (1 is top priority.)

☐ **1** My goal is to talk with people openly and honestly and encourage them to do the same with me.

☐ **2** I receive the required training to do my job; I fully understand what is to be done.

☐ **3** I have the required technical competence as well as the ability to work well with others.

☐ **4** My team leader's expectations are realistic and specific for the team.

☐ **5** Ownership is crucial to team building so I am involved in problem solving whenever possible.

☐ **6** While conflict in groups is normal, I work hard to resolve it quickly so it won't become destructive.

☐ **7** I work hard at developing trust and confidence in the process of growing a team.

☐ **8** When I see people working together, I provide positive feedback to reinforce their behavior.

☐ **9** I seek out ways to help other team members get to know each other better, which helps them build their respect for each other.

☐ **10** Team members regularly assess the team's growth compared to where we think it should be.

NOTES

Chapter 8
A Team Process-Improvement Model

Key Points

- 12 steps for improving your team process
- 3 levels of customer satisfaction: expected quality, specifications, and exciting quality
- Tools that will help you through each step of the 12-step model for daily management

This chapter examines a twelve-step, process-improvement model (see Figure 8-1). Using the proper tools and working together will contribute to the building and bonding of teams. This chapter is not focused on the growth of teams but on the work of teams in improving their processes. The purpose of each of the twelve steps will be explained in detail. This chapter introduces a number of tools, however, not all of the tools are explained. In-depth descriptions on the use of each tool can be found in The Memory Jogger™, The Memory Jogger™ II, and The Memory Jogger Plus+®. Another source, A Guide to Graphical Problem-Solving Processes, briefly describes the tools that are discussed in this chapter. For information on how to facilitate the use of the tools in a team setting, consult the Coach's Guide to The Memory Jogger™ II, or The Team Memory Jogger™.

12 Steps for Improving Your Team Process

The daily improvement process outlined in the following 12 steps follows the Plan, Do, Check, Act cycle. These steps were developed after researching a variety of successful problem-solving organizations.

Step 1
Know your organization. (See Figure 8-2.) Organizations start in the model by looking at their organization to understand what the organization does, what its values are, and the visions it brings to opportunity. Organizations should look at the strategic objectives of their enterprise, their current operational plans, where the organization is heading,

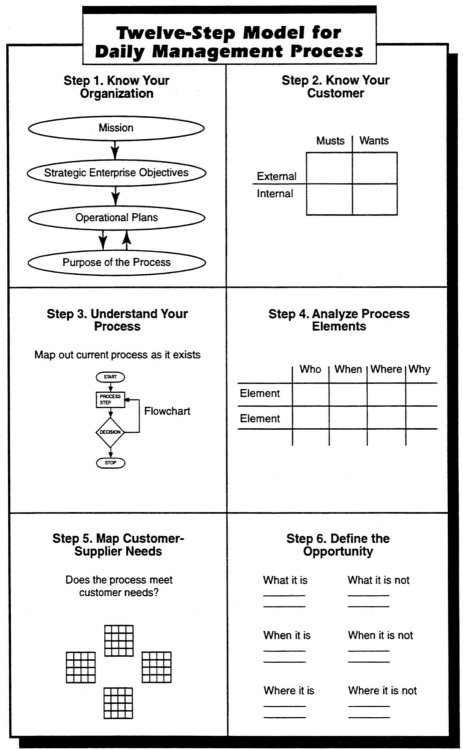

Figure 8-1

© 1991 by GOAL/QPC, Hoffherr, Moran

Twelve-Step Model for Daily Management Process

Step 7. Analyze Improvement Opportunities

Cause and Effect Diagram

People   Procedures

Effect

Policies   Equipment

Step 8. Synthesize the Causes

Pareto Chart   Force Field Diagram

Pick the most important cause to work on

Step 9. Synthesize the Opportunity

Run Chart   Check Sheet

Control Chart   Graphics

Upper Control Limit
x̄
Lower Control Limit

Step 10. Generate Solutions

Solution and Effect Tree   Matrix Diagram

Prioritize solutions

Step 11. Implement Solutions

Gantt Chart of Tasks   Process Decision Program Chart

Step 12. Standardize and Maintain

Standardize and hold the gain

S
Standardize

S
Act

D
Do

Check
C

Flowchart new process

START

PROCESS STEP

DECISION

STOP

Upper Control Limit
x̄
Lower Control Limit

Control Chart

© 1991 by GOAL/QPC, Hoffherr, Moran

Figure 8-1 *Continued*

where it would like to head, where it should be in the next year, and in the next 3–5 years. Once organizations feel confident that teams are aware of these values and understand the underlying concepts, (which are not usually verbalized), they should define the real purpose of each process in the organization. Too often, organizations forget to think about the *purpose* of their processes. For instance, if you were asked to drill a hole, without further instruction, how would you do it? You don't know your purpose in drilling a hole, so you cannot go about the task unless you ask more questions or . . . you guess! Perhaps you should use a drill for the task. Electric or hand drill? Already you have identified and narrowed your choices for accomplishing this task, though you don't know the reason for drilling a hole yet. In many problem-solving models, teams start to work on a very specific process that they feel is broken. This "drill a hole" process, for which the purpose is yet unknown, exists in many organizations!

Figure 8-2 Twelve-Step Model

Say instead that you were asked to make a hole. Within the context of a larger task, this may make a lot more sense. You may think of using a hammer, drill, shovel, wrecking ball! The purpose becomes more clear. If you were asked to create a void, what image does your mind evoke? The image is a little different from the drill. These different statements are hierarchical in accomplishing a basic purpose. When people attempt to solve problems, they need to keep a broad focus in mind. For instance, rather than say "Let's make the best buggy whips we can make," the broader statement "Let's make the best starters we can make," allows people more room for creative thought and creative solutions. The process of identifying the real purpose of the task before organizations begin their problem solving can keep them from solving the wrong problem. One of the key steps in improving a process is to make sure that the problem has meaning and value to the overall mission and objectives of the organization.

Step 2
Know your customer. (See Figure 8-3.) Many teams do not fully understand who the customers of their processes are or what their customers want. In the twelve-step improvement process, teams can focus on their external and internal customers. In our experience with teams, 20 percent of their customers were external, and 80 percent were internal customers. Team members will work with each other in focusing on customer-supplier relationships when they see the value of these relationships.

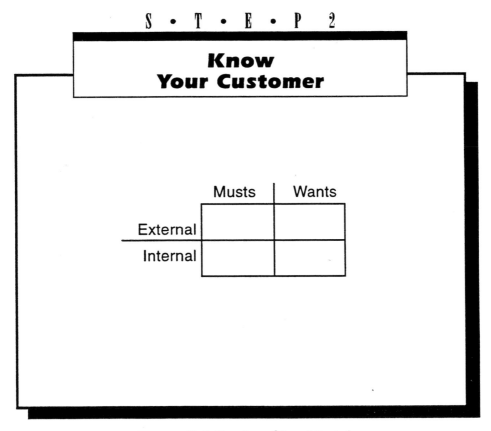

Figure 8-3 Twelve-Step Model

Internal and external customers have expectations that a specific type of product or service will fulfill their needs in a specific way. All customers, whether internal or external, require these "expected qualities" to be present, yet: 1) Customers have difficulty articulating what the "expected qualities" are, and 2) They assume the team knows the process well enough that it will understand their needs and design into the product or service the qualities that they expect. For example, if you are making a presentation with an overhead projector, the technically-minded people in your audience will assume it is UL approved and that you won't be zapped by a power surge. However, if you were asked what type of projector you needed for your presentation, you would most likely specify a brand name or another characteristic, not that it be UL approved. You assume all overhead projectors are UL approved.

As a team, members need to determine what qualities their customers are expecting. Many customers ask for qualities that are really specifications, qualities that, if not included, do not affect the function or integrity of the product or service. One of the best models that deals with teams illustrates three levels of customer satisfaction (Figure 8-4). This model was developed by Noriake Kano. He specifically deals with three different types of quality: expected quality, specifications, and exciting quality.

Figure 8-4

Expected qualities must be present in the product or service or people won't buy it. For instance, if your organization is presenting a training program with audience participation, the room needs to be the right size, set up to accommodate the number of people expected, and the presenters will need the right equipment to share information with the audience. If all these things are done correctly, it doesn't mean the people in the audience will be satisfied with the presentation. They expect that the room will be the right size, enough chairs will be set up for everyone, and the presenters will get their hands on the right equipment. Let's say the audience is satisfied with the presentation, except for two points. They would like to break for lunch for one hour instead of 20 minutes, and they would like time to ask questions. Kano refers to this this type of request as customer specifications.

A story that explains the "specifications" element of Kano's model concerns a fellow who drove to a shopping mall on his lunch break, and walked into a pet store. There was a parrot sitting in a cage quoting Shakespeare. Any play by Shakespeare the man mentioned, this parrot could repeat a quote from. He asked the store owner how much the parrot cost. The owner replied, "A thousand dollars with the cage." The man said he had a cage at home and again asked how much the parrot cost.

"Nine hundred dollars and ninety-nine cents" came the owner's reply.

So the man bought the parrot, took it home, and put it in the cage. Three days later he returned to the pet store and complained that the bird hadn't said a word in three days. The man said he read the bird Shakespeare, asked it if it wanted a cracker, and continued to talk to the bird for four hours. The bird said nothing! The store owner's response was, "He doesn't quote anything until he runs up the ladder."

"How much for the ladder?" the man asked.

"Ninety-nine, ninety nine" was the store owner's prompt response. The man bought the ladder, and three days later returned to the store.

"That bird still hasn't said a word" he complained loudly.

"Well, after he runs up the ladder, he looks at himself in the mirror, right?" the store owner asked.

"How much for the mirror?"

"Ninety-nine, ninety nine" the store owner shot back. The man bought the mirror, took it home, put it in the cage, and waited. But the bird still didn't talk. The man went directly to the store.

"Well, the parrot runs up the ladder, looks in the mirror, and still says nothing."

"What? It doesn't ring a bell?" asked the store owner.

The man bought a bell for another $99.99. He went home with the bell and put it in the cage with the parrot. Not even a syllable from the parrot. The man returned to the store furious and loudly complained to the owner.

"Of course, it loves to blow a whistle just before it speaks," the owner said. One last try the man assured himself and paid the owner $99.99. He returned home to the parrot and placed the whistle in the cage. There was an immediate flurry of activity in the cage and the parrot ran up the ladder, looked in the mirror, rang the bell, blew the whistle, finally said something, and promptly fell over dead. The man stormed back to the store where he proclaimed to the store owner that the bird finally spoke. Of course, the parrot's last words were "You forgot the bird seed!"

This is too often what people do to their customers. They spend so much time trying to "wow" their customers with bells and whistles that they don't meet their basic needs. In the improvement process it is imperative to first get teams to understand who their customers are and to identify their needs.

The third type of quality that Dr. Kano describes in his model are those qualities of a product or service that really excite (or wow) customers. It is important that teams understand what must be present to meet their customers' needs, what qualities or specifications customers want, and the types of qualities that will "wow" their customers.

Far too often people try to overcome a lack of process, or a very poor process, with bells and whistles because they can deliver them, instead of measuring what is important to their customers. Teams should examine their processes, identify who the customers of their processes are, identify the qualities their customers expect, and intelligently speculate what qualities may excite them.

Step 3
Understand your process. (See Figure 8-5.) The next step in the daily improvement process is to map out a current process as it exists. The flowchart is a good tool for this. One problem that many people have when they first begin to flowchart is that they want to get down to the *minute* details. They want to look, in detail, at each, step, in, the, process. What happens is they wind up with a flowchart that wraps around the room several times! They could spend months detailing their process with little value for their work. Before people construct a detailed flowchart, they should take a *macro, big picture* look at the process and map it out in 8 to 10 major steps. Don't get into too much detail this early in the flowcharting process. After a team has identified potentially significant areas, then is the time to get into more detail.

At this time, before getting detailed, it's a good idea for the team to review whether their current processes are aligned with their purposes, and whether the purposes match their customers' needs. Processes that are in place to accomplish this function are called *critical processes.*

By flowcharting the whole process at the broadest levels, a team has a significant advantage. Flowcharting allows a team to gather just the data it needs, rather than first gathering data on the whole process, and then focusing on the significant areas. It can be helpful to teams to know that there are four key attributes of any process. Processes:

- Are repeatable
- Occur over time
- Can be mapped
- Produce measurable results

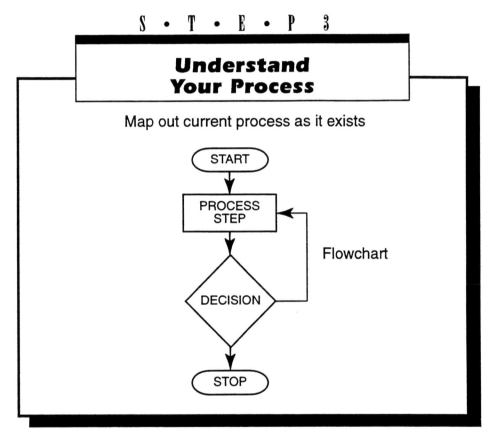

Figure 8-5 Twelve-Step Model

Are the results of your team's process necessarily what it wants? Perhaps not! A process at one company we worked with had an outcome of 7.2 cut hands per month. The company was not in the hand-cut industry. They made widgets. When we first started looking at the process, it produced 25 cut hands per month. Since the team has been working on improving its process, it has lowered the number of cut hands significantly, although it hasn't reached zero yet. The team continues to make progress. The point is that this company followed a process: it was repeatable, measurable, could be mapped, and occurred over time.

Frequently, people have similar developments in their current process. The similarity is that normally there are two, three, four or more processes "bundled together," which people at first view as only one process. To separate the "bundled" processes and see them all, flow-charting the process is the right place to begin. With a macro picture of a process, it is possible to identify all of the different processes that are rolled into the broader process. The act of flowcharting forces a team to step back and ask what the true task or purpose of its process is. Flowcharting allows a team to approach its process on a visual level: a team can bring abstract concepts into concrete shapes and tasks, place the tasks in an order of occurrence, which may illustrate the relationships between tasks, and get a snapshot of what is really happening in the process. With a shared picture of the process, team members can more easily talk about the process, and develop questions that will help the team to match the purpose of the process to customer needs. Some common questions that any team may form in flowcharting its process include: "In what part of the process is the problem occurring?" "Can some steps in the process be moved or eliminated?" "Where should we concentrate our efforts to make improvements?"

A Little More Information on Flowcharts
(adapted from The Memory Jogger™)

A flowchart is a pictorial representation showing all the steps in a process. Flowcharts can be useful for examining how various steps in a process are related to each other. For example, you can choose to flowchart a simple process, such as how meetings are arranged with your team members, or you could flowchart a more complex process, such as how your team will create a whole new process for delivering a new service. There are four basic symbols used to create a flowchart: 1) the oval, which represents the start and end of a process, 2) the rectangle, which represents an activity or operation in a process, 3) a diamond, which represents decision and inspection points in a process flow (decision follows either a "yes" or "no" path), and 4) a flowline, which connects the elements in a process. Flowcharts can be applied to anything from the travels of an invoice or the flow of materials, to the steps in making a sale or servicing a product.

Step 4
Analyze process elements. (See Figure 8-6.) After identifying the major process elements it is time to begin to analyze them. Ask questions such as "Who owns this element of the process?" "Who is performing or acting on this element of the process?" "When does this element occur?" "What takes place, why is it done, where is it done?" It is important to identify who owns the process element, and who performs or acts on the process element. The owner is the person who can decide to make changes, and has the last word on whether a process will be improved or left as it is. The person who is actually performing or acting on the element of the process is the most knowledgeable of its function, performance, and status.

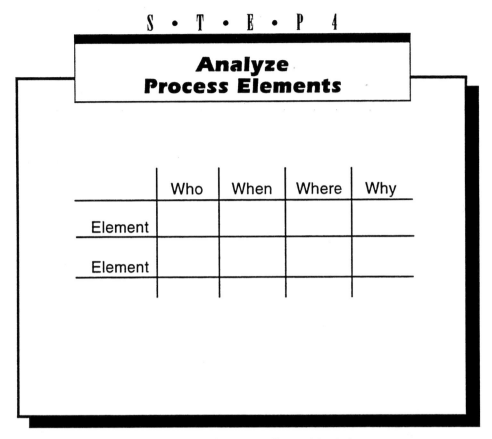

Figure 8-6 Twelve-Step Model

The purpose of spending this initial time on analyzing a process, instead of just starting with a problem to fix, is to address the correct problem. Normally, problem-solving models encourage people to "fix" before looking at the ramifications of a change in the process.

If a team hasn't jumped in and started to do anything yet, (the team is flowcharting its process), there is often tremendous pressure from management to break out of the twelve-step process and "just fix the problem!" It is important to realize that the twelve-step model is not just a problem-solving model, it is a process improvement model.

The initial identification of the elements in a process allows teams to ask whether each element is adding value to the process. Team members can dispute whether: "Is it an internal focus that is designed to catch mistakes or is it an internal focus that has been built into the process over the years?" "Is it an external focus?" "Is it designed to satisfy customers?" Waste in a process can be very difficult to identify and even more difficult to eliminate. A system has a vast inertia and dynamic of its own. Just changing a system without planning for the impact will produce very few long-lasting, positive changes, if any!

One example of how waste can be built into a system, without being identified, follows in the next paragraph. The names in the story have been made up, the story itself is true.

It was a new city for Tom Langley. And a new start. Tom had just accepted a new job and he was excited about his new career. On his first day at "Quality One," he found a three-inch thick report laying on top of his desk. After flipping through it, he set it aside. It didn't seem relevant at the time. The next week, a new report was put on his desk. This went on for six weeks before he finally realized this report might be unneeded, at least for him. He found out that the report had been generated for more than two years. It was initially generated because of a particular problem, which had come to pass. The person who was generating the report, Sylvia, was spending almost three days a week generating the report! Sylvia came in on Sundays, double time, for four hours, to run the report and distribute it to 13 people. With further investigation with the people who received the report, Tom found that no one used it, although each person said it contained so much good data. This report had been generated to address one specific problem, yet it had stayed in the system because no one questioned it. On closer inspection, and by asking "Does this report have an internal or external focus?" the recipients of the report determined its focus was internal. When they questioned whether the report had added value, they could answer with a resounding "No!". By eliminating this report, Sylvia now had more time to perform the real functions of her job. Everyone was amazed how they had overlooked this waste in the system. They congratulated Tom on recognizing it and speaking up.

It takes time to sit down and evaluate the individual elements of a process, however, it is much less time consuming than starting with a detailed flowcharting process, or fighting fire after fire. Doing a macro analysis can be important for keeping a team from following the traditional path of studying the problem and becoming Data Rich and Information Poor (the DRIP syndrome). The initial identification and analysis of the elements of a process will provide teams with a base for constructing a more detailed flowchart.

Detailed-level flowcharting becomes appropriate at this point on the process element that was identified as having the largest potential for improvement, based on the team's success criteria. Detailed flowcharting cannot be done sitting around a table, too many steps and decisions in the process may be overlooked. To flowchart the elements of a process accurately, someone must observe and write down all of the steps that occur in that element of the process. Additional information is often captured at this time, such as the amount of time a step requires, the distance something travels, how long something waits, and other pertinent information about the process.

Step 5
Map customer-supplier needs. (See Figure 8-7.) This step of the daily improvement process is to begin to look at how to relate the elements of a process back to customer needs. Teams often have difficulty fitting their process into the overall picture of the organization. By checking the process with customer needs, real relationships are revealed, if they exist. Using this process, teams should have identified a number of places to begin focusing on. The next step is to map the customer-supplier relationship. The customer-supplier map is described in

detail in Chapter 3 and Chapter 8 of *Daily Management: A System for Individual and Organizational Optimization.* This mapping process allows teams to examine two types of customers: primary and secondary.

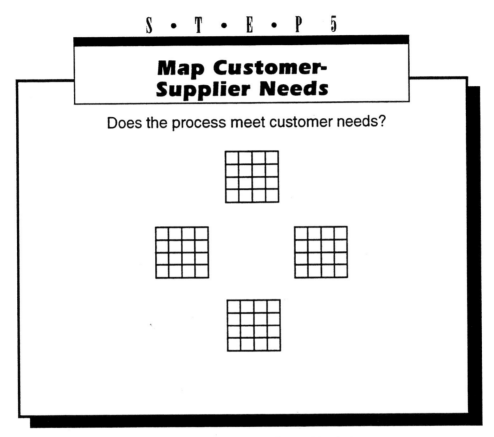

Figure 8-7 Twelve-Step Model

On most teams, at least 70 percent of the output goes to one customer. This is a primary customer. Teams should also define the primary *supplier* of its input. There are frequently secondary suppliers as well. The mapping process begins with the flowchart elements in the macro process flow. Measures for quality to meet customer needs should be listed. A comparison is done both by the team and its customers on how well each element is meeting each measurable and whether these measurables are meeting the needs of customers. This analysis identifies areas for continual improvement and areas for optimization and standardization. This process also helps to identify areas of waste in the process. Another benefit of this process is identification of real customer needs that have been overlooked in the current process.

There are two different types of process improvement opportunities. One type addresses those areas where good things have occurred. Too often these areas of opportunity are overlooked in favor of areas with perceived problems. Spending resources on ensuring the continuation of positives is at least as beneficial as spending resources on areas that appear to have problems. Frequently what happens is that management will take its resources off projects they are doing well, and put them on projects that are going badly. Over a period of time these good areas deteriorate and the bad areas temporarily improve. This pendulum cycle continues unabated until the team gets frustrated and stops functioning effectively. After a period of time, employees can almost tell you when a problem will reoccur.

To prevent this pendulum action, teams should focus on accepting the good areas and continue their maintenance through standardization, and work on the areas that will require major process improvement efforts. The customer-supplier map ties together the process and the needs of the customers of the process.

Step 6

Define the opportunity. (See Figure 8-8.) The next step of the daily improvement process is to do some very basic problem analysis by asking such questions as "What is happening?" "What is not happening?" "When is it happening?" "When is it not happening?" And so forth. Teams will begin to get some details, and should try to put some definition around what is really going on before asking for resources to improve a particular element of the process. This questioning technique is based on the work of Kepner-Tragoe.

It is amazing how often simple questions can solve complex problems. Many people tend to do this instinctively without realizing that they are actually doing basic problem identification. For instance, when people take their cars to be serviced, very few people tell the mechanic to "Just fix the car." A response to a statement like that might be "Just leave your credit card here. We'll call you in a few days when the car is fixed." Instead, most people will say something like "My front brakes squeak when it rains." This statement provides the mechanic with much more information. Yet when people approach problems to solve them as a team, they sometimes forget to ask simple questions to define the problem that everyone agrees *is* the problem!

Step 7

Analyze improvement opportunities. (See Figure 8-9.) The purpose of this step is to get to the root causes of a problem. A powerful tool to use for in-depth problem analysis is the cause and effect diagram (or fishbone). The value of this tool is that it provides teams with a non-threatening methodology to get to the root causes of what's going wrong in a process, without pointing blame at individuals. This particular tool is handy when there is a known effect and a team can work through the possible causes. When teams are working on a problem that is still being improved, teams may want to use another tool to more effectively standardize the gain.

S • T • E • P   6

Define
the Opportunity

What it is   What it is not
_____   _____

_____   _____

When it is   When it is not
_____   _____

_____   _____

Where it is   Where it is not
_____   _____

_____   _____

Figure 8-8 Twelve-Step Model

A Little More Information on Cause & Effect Diagrams
(excerpt from The Memory Jogger™)

The cause and effect diagram was developed to represent the relationship between some "effect" and all the possible "causes" influencing it. The effect or problem is stated on the right side of the chart and the major influences or "causes" are listed to the left. Diagrams that are well-detailed will take on the shape of a fish skeleton, hence the name fishbone diagram.

Fishbone diagrams are drawn to clearly illustrate the various causes affecting a process by sorting out and relating the causes. For every effect there are likely to be several major categories of causes. The major causes might be summarized under four categories: 1) people, 2) machines, 3) methods, and 4) materials. In administrative areas, the categories people, policies, procedures, and plant may be more appropriate. These categories are only suggestions, teams may use any major category that emerges or helps them to think creatively.

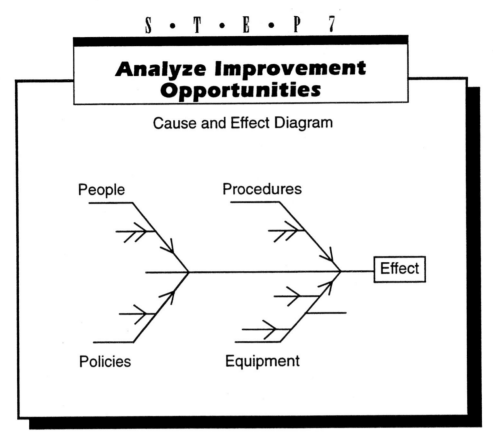

Figure 8-9 Twelve-Step Model

Step 8
Synthesizing the causes. (See Figure 8-10.) In this step, the most likely causes are identified. There are a number of tools that are frequently used to identify these opportunities, including the Pareto Chart, which illustrates the principle that 80 percent of the symptoms are a result of 20 percent of the causes. Force field diagrams allow teams to analyze a problem or an opportunity by the forces that are driving a particular event toward happening and the forces that are preventing that event from occurring. The force field diagram is a powerful tool, (but simple to construct and understand), that teams tend to overlook. Another tool that is very useful is the selection grid, which enables teams to focus on only the issues that they can influence. The selection grid allows teams to give priority to all the potential issues they can work on, based on whatever criteria they have assigned. The selection grid is described in the book *A Guide to Graphical Problem-Solving Processes* by Russell Benson, John Moran, and Richard Talbot.

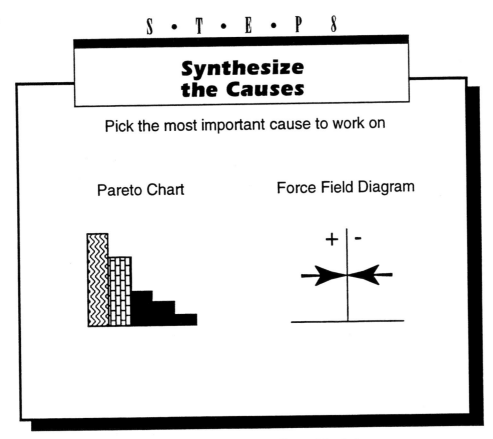

Figure 8-10 Twelve-Step Model

A Little More Information on Force Field Diagrams
(excerpt from The Memory Jogger™*)*

How does change occur, either personally or organizationally? It's a dynamic process. It suggests movement, either from "time A" to "time B" or "condition x" to "condition y," and so on.Where does the energy for this "movement" come from? One approach is to view change as the result of a struggle between forces that are seeking to upset the status quo. This view is taken in the work of Kurt Lewin, who developed a technique called "force field analysis." In Lewin's work, he proposes that "driving forces" move a situation toward change while "restraining forces" block that movement. When there is no change, the opposing forces are equal or the restraining forces are too strong to allow movement. Consider the practical example of "losing weight":

Driving Forces	**Restraining Forces**
Health threat	Lack of time
Cultural obsession with thinness	Genetic traits
Plenty of thin role models	Unsympathetic friends & family
Embarassment	Lack of money for exercise
Negative self-image	Lack of interest
Positive attitude toward exercise	Bad advice
Lack of temptation	Years of bad eating habits
Clothes don't fit	Amount of sugar in any prepared food

If the restraining forces are stronger than the driving forces, then the desired change will not happen. It stands to reason that some change (losing weight) will occur if the driving forces are more powerful than the restraining forces. How can force field analysis help teams make changes?

- Constructing "force fields" makes people think together about all the facets of a desired change.
- Constructing "force fields" encourages people to agree on the relative priority of factors on each side of the "balance sheet."
- Constructing "force fields" provides a starting point for people to take action.

A Little More Information on Pareto Charts
(adapted from The Memory Jogger™*)*

Pareto charts are a special form of vertical bar graphs that help teams determine which problems to solve in what order. Creating a Pareto chart based on either check sheets or other forms of data collection help teams direct their attention and efforts to the true problems. Teams will generally gain more by working on the tallest bar than tackling the smaller bar. Pareto charts can be used in four ways:

1. To analyze different groupings of data. For example, by product, by department, by time of year. For example, teams can use Pareto charts to compare the frequency of several types of defects, in one or many products, the frequency of defects during certain months of the year, and the frequency of defects on different shifts.
2. To identify the most important problems by using different measurement scales, such as frequency and cost in collecting data. The most frequent problems are not always the most costly! For example, teams can use Pareto charts to show the frequency of customer complaints across company departments or functions, and the dollar costs associated with installing new equipment to lower the number of customer complaints in a particular department.
3. To measure the impact of changes made in a process, tracking measurements before and after each change. For example, teams can use Pareto charts to show the change in percentage or frequency of incorrect invoices for different services, products, or supplies before installing an automated computer system and after installation; and again before one-on-one staff training and after training.

4. To break down broad outcomes/objects into more and more specific events or components. For example, teams can use Pareto charts to compare the number of personal injuries in the workplace with specific areas of the body (eyes, backs, hands). Then, teams can look at the different causes of eye, back, and/or hand injuries and graph the frequency of the injury with its cause.

Step 9
Synthesizing the opportunity. (See Figure 8-11.) The purpose of this step is to determine what is currently happening, what is being observed, and what the biggest areas of opportunity are, based on the data that is available.

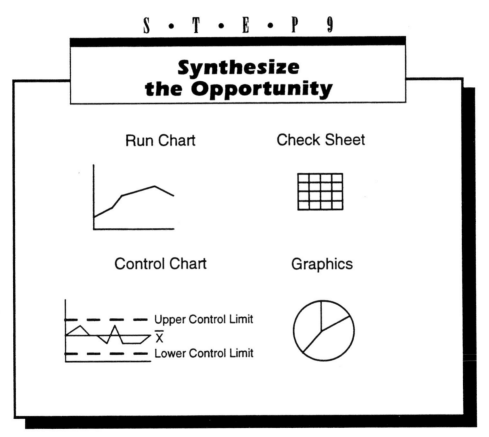

Figure 8-11 Twelve-Step Model

This is the point in the improvement process where data collection begins. By this time, teams should know what information is required to verify the size and the dimensions of the opportunity. Teams determine what data needs to be gathered, what type of data it is, and what they will do with the data after they have gathered it. After teams have answered these questions, they can determine how to most effectively gather the data. Teams should ask questions such as "Can we use as simple a tool as the check sheet?" "Can we use the run chart?" "The histogram?" "Control charts?" "Can we use a simple graphic tool, or do we have to get into more complex tools?" "Do we need to get in-depth training?" "Do we need to review some tools?"

By answering these types of questions, teams are able to determine which data tool to use. Some of the most frequently used tools, as described in both *The Memory Jogger™* and *A Guide to Graphical Problem-Solving Processes* are run charts, check sheets, control charts, pie charts and bar graphs, histograms, and scatter diagrams. This is not a comprehensive list of available tools, however, these tools are the most frequently used in the early stages of a team culture. Very frequently, in-depth statistical tools are not needed at this stage, but they do become vital in Step 12 of this model.

A Little More Information on Check Sheets
(excerpt from The Memory Jogger™*)*

Check sheets are simply easy-to-understand forms that help teams to find out the frequency of an event or activity. Check sheets help teams begin the process of translating opinions into facts.

Tips for Constructing Check Sheets

- Determine the activity/event to be observed and how it will be measured and recorded. Everyone needs to look for the same thing.
- Agree on a time period to collect data. This can range from one hour to several weeks.
- Design a form that is clear and easy to use. Label columns clearly and leave adequate space for entering data.
- Collect data by recording the number of occurrences. Be honest and consistent.

A Little More Information on Histograms
(adapted from The Memory Jogger™*)*

Histograms, like Pareto charts, display the frequency of an event/activity in bar graph form. However, Pareto charts display only comparisons between frequency or cost and the characteristics of objects, components, activities, or outcomes. Histograms take measurement data like temperature or product dimensions, and display their distribution. This distribution is critical because we know that all repeated events will produce results that vary over time. Histograms reveal the amount of variation that any process has within it.

A Little More Information on Control Charts
(excerpt from The Memory Jogger™*)*

A control chart is simply a run chart with statistically determined upper (upper control limit) and possibly lower (lower control limit) lines drawn on either side of the process average. These limits are calculated by running a process untouched (that is, according to standard procedures but without any extra "tweaking" adjustments), taking samples, and plugging the sample averages into the appropriate formula. The sample averages can then be plotted onto a chart to determine whether any of the points fall between or outside of the limits or form unlikely patterns. If either of these happen, the process is said to be "out of control."

The fluctuation of the points within the limits results from variation built into the process. This results from common causes within the system (that is, design, choice of machine, preventive maintenance), and can only be affected by changing that system. However, points outside of the limits come from a special cause (that is, people errors, unplanned events, freak occurrences), that is not part of the way that the process normally operates, or from an unlikely combination of process steps. These special causes must be eliminated before the control chart can be used as a monitoring tool. Once this is done, the process would be "in control" and samples can be taken at regular intervals to make sure that the process doesn't fundamentally change. "Control" doesn't necessarily mean that the product or service will meet your needs. It only means that the process is consistent (may be consistently bad).

A Little More Information on Pie Charts
(excerpt from The Memory Jogger™*)*

Pie charts are graphs in which the entire circle represents 100% of the data to be displayed. The circle, or pie, is divided into percentage slices that clearly show the largest shares of data. Pie charts are useful in the same way as Pareto charts. Sometimes the pie chart is more useful because of its common use on TV or in newspapers. Be sure to clearly mark the subject matter, dates if needed, the percentages within the slices, and what each slice represents.

A Little More Information on Run Charts
(adapted from The Memory Jogger™*)*

Run charts are used to monitor a process to see whether or not the long-range average is changing, and if there are meaningful trends or shifts in the average. Data points are plotted on a graph in the order in which they become available. It is common to graph the results of a process such as employee absence from work, product delivery time, typographical errors, incoming phonecalls, or productivity as they vary over time. A danger in using run charts is the tendency to see every variation in data as important. The run chart, like the other charting tools, should be used to focus attention on truly vital changes in the process.

A Little More Information on Scatter Diagrams
(excerpt from The Memory Jogger™*)*

Scatter diagrams are used to study the possible relationship between one variable and another. They are used to test for possible cause and effect relationships, however, they cannot prove that one variable causes the other. Scatter diagrams are useful for determining whether a relationship exists and the strength of that relationship.

Scatter diagrams have a horizontal axis (x-axis), to represent the measurement values of one variable, and a vertical axis (y-axis), to represent the measurements of the second variable.

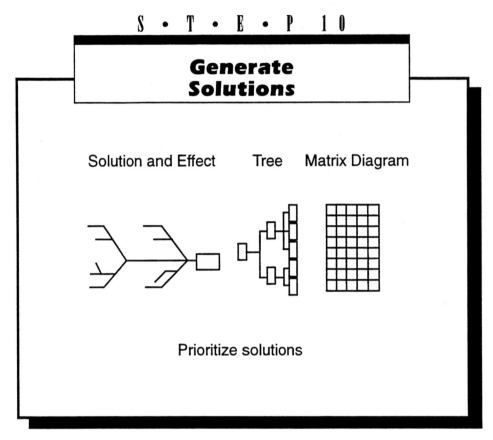

Figure 8-12 Twelve-Step Model

Step 10

Generate solutions. (See Figure 8-12.) The purpose of this step is to allow teams to generate a number of potential solutions to improve a process. If a team has only one solution to improve the process, the members do not understand the process. If the team has only one potential solution, it is a sign the team process itself needs to be readdressed.

There are a number of tools that work well to generate potential solutions, including brainstorming, the solution and effect diagram, and the tree diagram. The solution and effect diagram works very similarly to the cause and effect diagram. Teams should follow the six steps listed below when they are constructing solution and effect diagrams:

1. Make the desired effect a positive statement and place it in the box at the "head" of a cause and effect diagram.
2. Brainstorm possible solutions and place them into large categories.
3. Use a flow diagram (flowchart) to show where these potential solutions would be inserted into the process.
4. If the team is still uncovering potential causes, stop and go back to Step 7 of the process improvement model.

5. Answer the questions of who, what, when, where, why, and how for each of the potential solutions.
6. Pick one of the potential solutions, basing your choice on the answers to the above questions.

Use the tree diagram and prioritization matrices to develop the solution to the task level.

To ensure the solution really works, teams need to develop criteria for the solution. How will teams judge whether the solution is effective? What criteria does the team have for success? It's best to develop these criteria early in the process. The success criteria should be developed *before* any potential solutions so that teams can use match the criteria against each solution. The first ten steps of this model can be characterized as the Plan portion of the Plan, Do, Check, Act (PDCA) cycle, although each step incorporates the entire PDCA cycle within it as well.

Step 11
Implement solutions. (See Figure 8-13.) In this step, teams should develop a detailed implementation plan, including a timeline, measurables, tasks, responsibilities, and then use Dr. Deming's 14th point, "Go out and do it." Developing the greatest possible plan does no good if it is not implemented. This step can be characterized as the Do portion of the PDCA cycle. Following implementation, there is one last step to do.

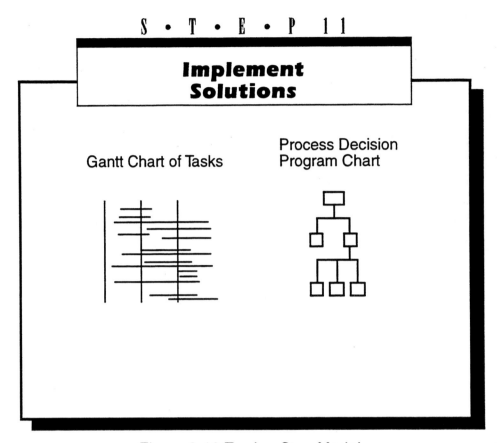

Figure 8-13 Twelve-Step Model

Step 12
Standardize and maintain. (See Figure 8-14.) From the point that an organization actually implements an improvement plan, the team needs to continue to monitor its effects. This step can be characterized as the Check portion of the PDCA cycle. If the improvement plan is accomplishing the desired effect, the organization should take action to standardize it and make sure it becomes the new way of doing things. This is known as the Standardize, Do, Check, Act (SDCA) cycle. Data should be collected and monitored to ensure that the new process continues to function as implemented. In addition, the new process should be checked to ensure that it continues to meet customer needs.

If the new process does not produce the effect that the organization wanted, the organization should continue to use the PDCA cycle and return to the process improvement step that fits the deficiency. Teams might not have to return to the beginning, they may be able to jump in at Step 5, 6, or 7, as they use the PDCA cycle and a focused problem-solving methodology. At times, teams may be able to make a major improvement instead of a small improvement.

The point of presenting this process improvement model is to convey the idea that teams will have a number of steps to follow through on, and that there are a number of tools they can use to accomplish their tasks in each step. The 12-step model for process improvement is a tool for helping teams to analyze a problem and its effect on customers. After so much work, teams will want to be absolutely sure that the *right* process has been improved!

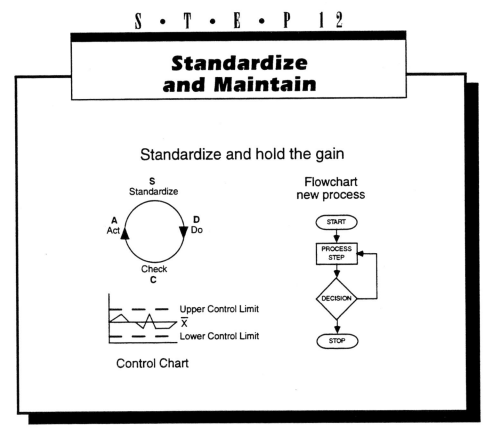

Figure 8-14 Twelve-Step Model

Exercise 12 Instructions

How Well Do You Know the Basic Quality Tools?

Purpose

The focus of this exercise is to determine each team member's level of knowledge of the tools that are recommended in the 12-step model for team process improvement.

Preparation

- Give each participant a copy of the exercise.
- Provide enough pens and pencils for everyone.
- Lay out several multicolored felt tip markers for anyone to use.
- Set up a flip chart or writing board in the area.

Process

- Ask participants to rate their personal knowledge of the listed tools.
- Help participants to construct a Pareto chart of the responses for each tool. (Consult *The Memory Jogger*™ or *The Memory Jogger*™ *II* on how to construct this tool.) Allow 30 minutes to explain the construction of a Pareto chart and for "walking" the group through each step.
- Allow participants 5 minutes to complete the form for Exercise 12.

Discussion

- Assure participants that they will learn to use these tools as they are needed.
- Assure participants that these tools will facilitate the team process.

▶ Time required: 30–45 minutes total
▶ Group size: Optimum is 4–9 people, but up to 20 people is acceptable

Exercise 12
How Well Do You Know the
Basic Quality Tools?

Rate yourself.

Tool	Knowledge of Tool				
	Low				High
1. Customer Matrix	1	2	3	4	5
2. Flowchart	1	2	3	4	5
3. Cause and Effect Diagram	1	2	3	4	5
4. Customer-Supplier Map	1	2	3	4	5
5. Nominal Group Technique (NGT)	1	2	3	4	5
6. Pareto Chart	1	2	3	4	5
7. Check Sheet	1	2	3	4	5
8. Run Chart	1	2	3	4	5
9. Histogram	1	2	3	4	5
10. Scatter Diagram	1	2	3	4	5
11. Pie Chart	1	2	3	4	5
12. Bar Graph	1	2	3	4	5
13. Control Chart	1	2	3	4	5
14. Solution and Effect Diagram	1	2	3	4	5
15. Force Field Diagram	1	2	3	4	5
16. Tree Diagram	1	2	3	4	5
17. Gantt Chart	1	2	3	4	5
18. Matrix Diagram	1	2	3	4	5
19. Process Decision Program Chart	1	2	3	4	5
20. Plan, Do, Check, Act Cycle	1	2	3	4	5
21. Standardize, Do, Check, Act Cycle	1	2	3	4	5

Exercise 13 Instructions

What are Your Customers' Needs?

Purpose

The purpose of this exercise is to introduce the customer needs matrix to problem-solving teams. This tool is the most effective when it is introduced to teams on an as-needed basis. There are several ways to generate a list of customer needs. For information on how participants can be directed in generating a list of customer needs, refer to *Making Daily Management Work: A Perspective for Leaders and Managers*, pages 63–67.

Preparation

- Give each participant a copy of the exercise.
- Provide enough pens and pencils for everyone.
- Lay out several multicolored felt tip markers for anyone to use.
- Set up a flip chart or writing board in the area.

Process

- Using a flip chart, discuss the difference between internal and external customers.
- Complete a list of internal and external customers for your organization.
- Post the list for team participants.
- Ask participants to complete the matrix for one internal customer and one external customer.

Discussion

- Emphasize that the musts and wants the participants have listed in the matrix need to be verified with their customers.

▶ Time required: 30–45 minutes total
▶ Group size: Optimum is 4–9 people, but up to 20 people is acceptable

Exercise 13
What Are Your Customers' Needs?

Construct a matrix.

	Musts	Wants
Internal		
External		

Exercise 14 Instructions

What is Your Team's Process for Solving Problems?

Purpose

The purpose of this exercise is to introduce the flowchart to problem-solving teams. This tool is most effective if introduced to teams on an as-needed basis. For details on how to construct this tool, reference *The Memory Jogger™*, *The Memory Jogger™ II,* or *A Guide to Graphical Problem Solving Processes*. For details on how to facilitate the construction and use of this tool, reference the *Coach's Guide to The Memory Jogger™ II.*

Preparation

- Give each participant a copy of the exercise.
- Provide enough pens and pencils for everyone.
- Lay out several multicolored felt tip markers for anyone to use.
- Set up a flip chart or writing board in the area.

Process

- Introduce the four basic flowchart symbols to participants.
- Review with participants the example flowchart, "Turning on a Television."
- Ask participants to complete Exercise 14. They should flowchart the process of popping popcorn.

Discussion

- Discuss the different types of flowcharts (macro, detail, layout) and their uses.
- Emphasize to participants that to do a thorough job on a flowchart, the actual process must be observed.
- Discuss the values of the flowcharting process.
- Discuss the learnings of the group.

▶ Time required: 45–60 minutes total
▶ Group size: Optimum is 4–9 people, but up to 20 people is acceptable

Exercise 14
What Is Your Team's Process
for Solving Problems?

Using the symbols below,
flowchart a process for popping corn.

Flowchart Symbols

Oval (Start or Stop)	Rectangle (Activity or Operation)	Diamond (Decision Point)	Flowline (Connects Elements)

→ or ←

↓ or ↑

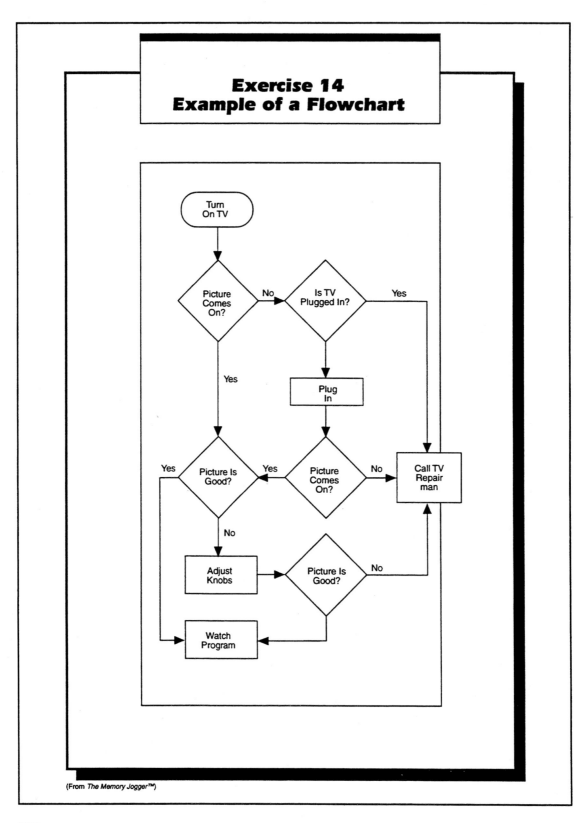

**Exercise 14
Example of a Flowchart**

(From *The Memory Jogger™*)

NOTES

Exercise 15 Instructions

What's the Problem? Use the Fishbone Diagram

Purpose

The purpose of this exercise is to introduce the flowchart to problem-solving teams. This tool is most effective if introduced to teams on an as-needed basis. For details on how to construct this tool, reference *The Memory Jogger*™, *The Memory Jogger*™ *II*, or *A Guide to Graphical Problem Solving Processes*. For details on how to facilitate the construction and use of this tool, reference the *Coach's Guide to The Memory Jogger*™ *II*.

Preparation
- Give each participant a copy of the exercise.
- Provide enough pens and pencils for everyone.
- Lay out several multicolored felt tip markers for anyone to use.
- Set up a flip chart or writing board in the area.

Process
- Explain to participants how to construct the cause & effect diagram.
- Give each participant a copy of the blank cause & effect diagram on "Video Recorder Will Not Play."
- Ask participants to complete the diagram by adding any other major categories as they come up.

Discussion
- Ask participants to describe what information they can derive from this diagram.
- Ask participants to describe possible uses for this tool in their process.
- Ask participants to describe the learnings they have derived from this tool.

▶ Time required: 30–45 minutes total
▶ Group size: Optimum is 4–9 people, but up to 20 people is acceptable

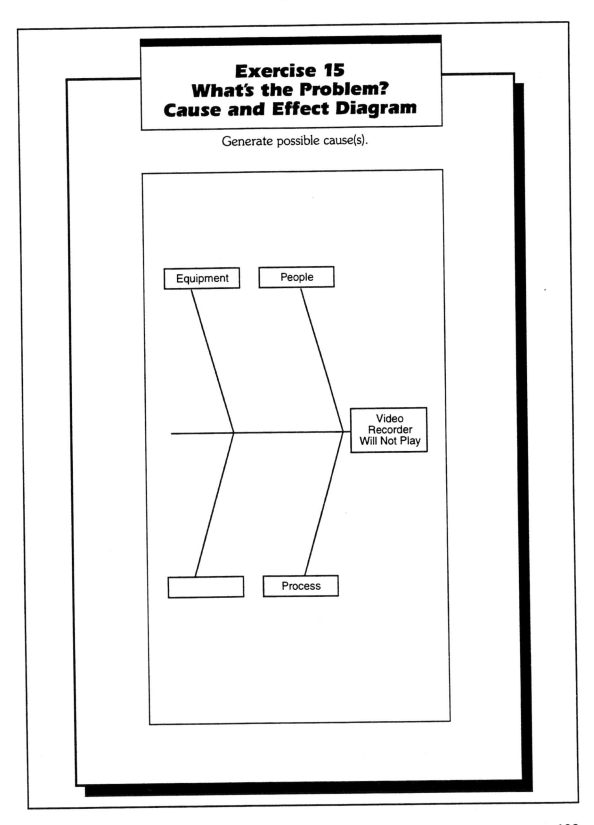

**Exercise 15
What's the Problem?
Cause and Effect Diagram**

Generate possible cause(s).

Equipment

People

Video
Recorder
Will Not Play

Process

Exercise 16 Instructions

How Do You Decide Which Cause is the Most Probable Root of the Problem? Try the Nominal Group Technique

Purpose

The purpose of this exercise is to introduce the nominal group technique to problem-solving teams. This tool is most effective if introduced to the team on an as-needed basis. For details on how to construct this tool, please reference *The Memory Jogger*™ or *The Memory Jogger*™ *II*. For details on how to facilitate the construction and use of this tool, reference the *Coach's Guide to The Memory Jogger*™ *II*.

Preparation

- Give each participant a copy of the exercise.
- Provide enough pens and pencils for everyone.
- Lay out several multicolored felt tip markers for anyone to use.
- Set up a flip chart or writing board in the area.

Process

- Explain the nominal group technique.
- Ask participants to use the nominal group technique to vote for the most probable cause of why the video recorder will not play (see Exercise 15).

Discussion

- Ask participants to describe what information they can derive from this technique.
- Ask participants to describe possible uses for this tool in their process.
- Ask participants to describe the learnings they have derived from this tool.

▶ Time required: 15–30 minutes total
▶ Group size: Optimum is 4–9 people, but up to 20 people is acceptable

Exercise 16
How Do You Decide Which Cause is the Most Probable Root of the Problem?

Try the nominal group technique.

Use the nominal group technique to vote for the most probable root cause for the "video recorder will not play" cause & effect diagram (Exercise 15).

Exercise 17 Instructions

How Does Your Team Move Beyond Speculation and Inference? Use Check Sheets

Purpose

The purpose of this exercise is to introduce the check sheet to problem-solving teams. This tool is most effective if introduced to the team on an as-needed basis. For details on how to construct this tool, please reference *The Memory Jogger™* or *The Memory Jogger™ II*. For details on how to facilitate the construction and use of this tool, reference the *Coach's Guide to The Memory Jogger™ II*.

Preparation

- Give each participant a copy of the exercise.
- Provide enough pens and pencils for everyone.
- Lay out several multicolored felt tip markers for anyone to use.
- Set up a flip chart or writing board in the area.

Process

- Ask participants to add the data in the columns and rows of the "big nuts and bolts check sheet."

Discussion

- What information can participants determine from the data collected?
- How would participants redesign this check sheet to gather more meaningful information?
- It is always a good idea to place dummy data into the check sheet to verify design before spending the resources to actually collect the data. It is easier to redesign the form than to recollect the data.
- Discuss the learnings of the group.

▶ Time required: 15–30 minutes total
▶ Group size: Optimum is 4–9 people, but up to 20 people is acceptable

Exercise 17
Big Nuts and Bolts
Check Sheet

How Does Your Team Move Beyond Speculation
and Inference? "In God we trust. All others use data!"
Use the check sheet.

Name _____   Effect _____
Date _____   Team _____

Project or Task	Start Date / End Date	Total Days Per Project	Walk-Ins	Staff	Meetings	Telephone	Noise	Errands	Travel	Other	Total
A			‖‖			‖		|		‖‖	
B				‖‖‖	|			‖‖‖			
C			‖‖		‖‖‖					‖	
D				|	‖‖			‖‖‖			
Total											

Exercise 18 Instructions

What's Happening Where and When? Try the Pareto Chart

Purpose

The purpose of this exercise is to introduce the Pareto Chart to problem-solving teams. This tool is most effective if introduced to the team on an as-needed basis. For details on how to construct this tool, please reference *The Memory Jogger™*, *The Memory Jogger™ II*, or *A Guide to Graphical Problem Solving Processes*. For details on how to facilitate the construction and use of this tool, reference the *Coach's Guide to The Memory Jogger™ II*.

Preparation

- ◌ Give each participant a copy of the exercise.
- ◌ Provide enough pens and pencils for everyone.
- ◌ Lay out several multicolored felt tip markers for anyone to use.
- ◌ Set up a flip chart or writing board in the area.

Process

- ◌ Explain to participants how to construct the Pareto chart.
- ◌ Give each participant a copy of the data of the "Ace Software Customer Complaints" and the blank form for the Pareto chart.
- ◌ Ask participants complete the Pareto chart.

Discussion

- ◌ Ask participants to describe what information they can derive from this chart.
- ◌ Ask participants to describe possible uses for this tool in their process.
- ◌ Ask participants to describe the learnings they have derived from this tool.

▶ Time required: 30–45 minutes total
▶ Group size: Optimum is 4–9 people, but up to 20 is acceptable

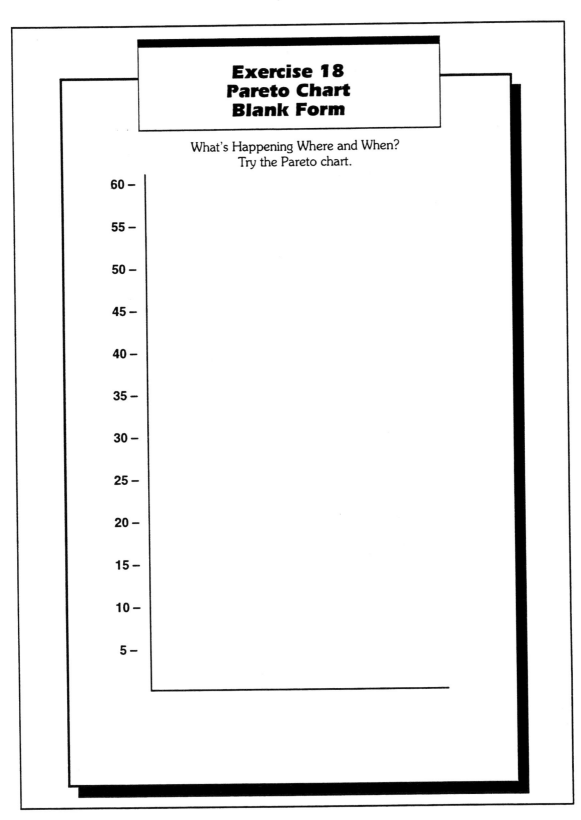

**Exercise 18
Pareto Chart
Blank Form**

What's Happening Where and When?
Try the Pareto chart.

60 –

55 –

50 –

45 –

40 –

35 –

30 –

25 –

20 –

15 –

10 –

5 –

Exercise 18
Data for Pareto Chart

Ace Software

Type	No. of Complaints
High Cost	12
Billing for Repeat Customer Engineer Visits	20
Walk-In Center	55
Performance Issues	50
Warranty Problems	5
Customer Needs Further Training	21
Incorrect Information on Bill	10
Incorrect Charges	18
Rude Staff Member	11
Other	2

Customer Complaints 10/1 - 3/31

NOTES

Exercise 19 Instructions

Give that Problem a Run for Its Money: The Run Chart

Purpose

The purpose of this exercise is to introduce the run chart to problem-solving teams. This tool is most effective if introduced to the team on an as-needed basis. For details on how to construct this tool, please reference *The Memory Jogger™*, *The Memory Jogger™ II*, or *A Guide to Graphical Problem Solving Processes*. For details on how to facilitate the construction and use of this tool, reference the *Coach's Guide to The Memory Jogger™ II*.

Preparation

- ○ Give each participant a copy of the exercise.
- ○ Provide enough pens and pencils for everyone.
- ○ Lay out several multicolored felt tip markers for anyone to use.
- ○ Set up a flip chart or writing board in the area.

Process

- ○ Explain to participants how to construct the run chart.
- ○ Give each participant a copy of the run chart data for admissions to Garden Memorial Hospital, and a copy of the "run chart, blank form."
- ○ Ask participants to plot the data and complete the run chart.
- ○ Tell participants that October 1 is a Tuesday.

Discussion

- ○ Ask participants to describe what information they can derive from this chart. (Wednesdays always have high admissions. Doctors took Wednesday afternoon off to admit patients. (Garden Memorial Hospital is primarily a surgical hospital.)
- ○ Ask participants to describe possible uses for this tool in their process.
- ○ Ask participants to describe the learnings they have derived from this tool.
- ○ The Run Chart exercise should be tied to the Histogram exercise. If the participants have completed the Histogram (Exercise 20) using these data, ask them to compare the results of the run chart and histogram to see what differences can be determined.

▶ Time required: 30–45 minutes total
▶ Group size: Optimum is 4–9 people, but up to 20 people is acceptable

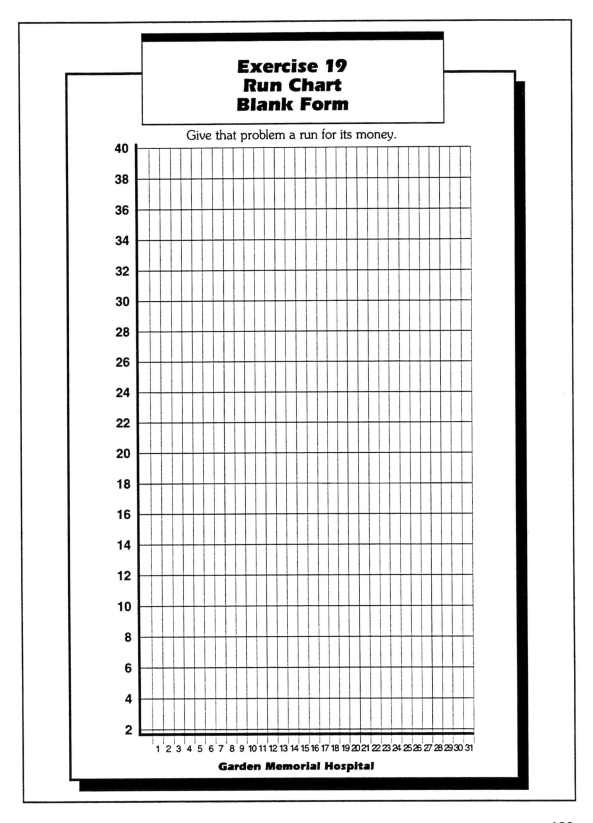

**Exercise 19
Run Chart
Blank Form**

Give that problem a run for its money.

Garden Memorial Hospital

Exercise 19
Data for Run Chart

The following data was collected on overall admissions to
Garden Memorial Hospital in October

October	No. of Admissions
1	28
2	34
3	25
4	29
5	15
6	16
7	26
8	28
9	34
10	28
11	24
12	10
13	16
14	22
15	26
16	39

October	No. of Admissions
17	25
18	26
19	12
20	20
21	31
22	32
23	36
24	24
25	22
26	16
27	20
28	23
29	22
30	34
31	22
31 days	765 admissions

Exercise 20 Instructions

What's the Range of Variation in that Process? The Histogram

Purpose

The purpose of this exercise is to introduce the histogram to problem-solving teams. This tool is most effective if introduced to the team on an as-needed basis. For details on how to construct this tool, please reference *The Memory Jogger™, The Memory Jogger™ II,* or *A Guide to Graphical Problem Solving Processes.* For details on how to facilitate the construction and use of this tool, reference the *Coach's Guide to The Memory Jogger™ II.*

Preparation

- ◌ Give each participant a copy of the exercise.
- ◌ Provide enough pens and pencils for everyone.
- ◌ Lay out several multicolored felt tip markers for anyone to use.
- ◌ Set up a flip chart or writing board in the area.

Process

- ◌ Explain to participants how to construct the histogram.
- ◌ Give each participant a copy of the histogram data of admissions to Garden Memorial Hospital, and a copy of the "histogram, blank form."
- ◌ Ask participants to complete the histogram looking at the six groups of categories.

Discussion

- ◌ Ask participants to describe what information they can derive from this chart. (The shape approximates a normal distribution.)
- ◌ Ask participants to describe possible uses for this tool in their process.
- ◌ Ask participants to describe the learnings they have derived from this tool.
- ◌ If the participants have completed the run chart using this data, ask them to compare the results of the run chart (Exercise 19) and the histogram to see what differences can be determined.

- ▶ Time required: 30–45 minutes total
- ▶ Group size: Optimum is 4–9 people, but up to 20 people is acceptable

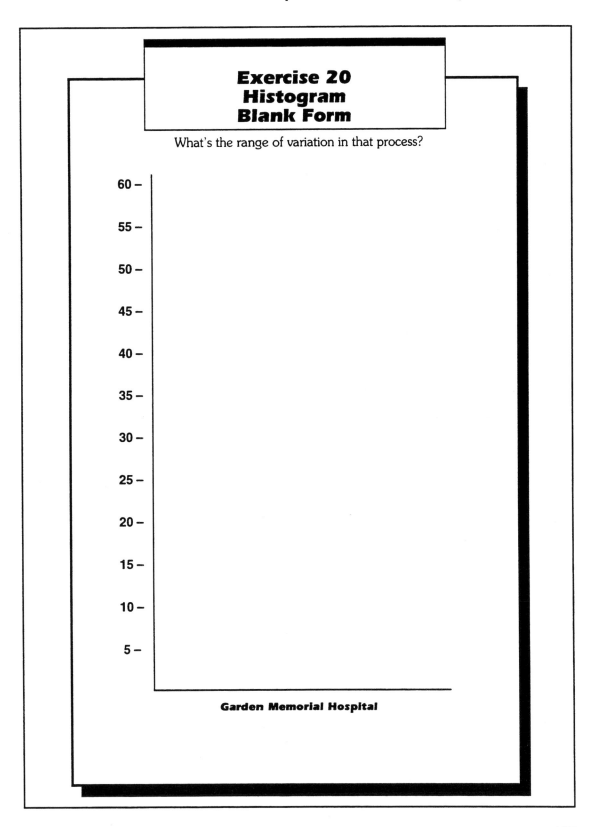

**Exercise 20
Histogram
Blank Form**

What's the range of variation in that process?

60 –

55 –

50 –

45 –

40 –

35 –

30 –

25 –

20 –

15 –

10 –

5 –

Garden Memorial Hospital

Exercise 20
Data for Histogram

The following data was collected on overall admissions to
Garden Memorial Hospital in October

October	No. of Admissions
1	28
2	34
3	25
4	29
5	15
6	16
7	26
8	28
9	34
10	28
11	24
12	10
13	16
14	22
15	26
16	39

October	No. of Admissions
17	25
18	26
19	12
20	20
21	31
22	32
23	36
24	24
25	22
26	16
27	20
28	23
29	22
30	34
31	22
31 days	765 admissions

NOTES

Exercise 21 Instructions

Is There a Correlation Between These Data? Scatter Diagrams

Purpose
The purpose of this exercise is to introduce the scatter diagram to problem-solving teams. This tool is most effective if introduced to the team on an as-needed basis. For details on how to construct this tool, please reference *The Memory Jogger™*, *The Memory Jogger™ II*, or *A Guide to Graphical Problem Solving Processes*. For details on how to facilitate the construction and use of this tool, reference the *Coach's Guide to The Memory Jogger™ II*.

Preparation
- ⊃ Give each participant a copy of the exercise.
- ⊃ Provide enough pens and pencils for everyone.
- ⊃ Lay out several multicolored felt tip markers for anyone to use.
- ⊃ Set up a flip chart or writing board in the area.

Process
- ⊃ Explain to participants how to construct the scatter diagram.
- ⊃ Give each participant a copy of the scatter diagram data on the Apex Hotel, and a copy of "scatter diagram, blank form."
- ⊃ Ask participants to complete the diagram.

Discussion
- ⊃ Ask participants to describe what information they can derive from the scatter diagram.
- ⊃ Ask participants to describe possible uses for this tool in their process.
- ⊃ Ask participants to describe the learnings they have derived from this tool.

▶ Time required: 30–45 minutes total
▶ Group size: Optimum is 4–9 people, but up to 20 people is acceptable

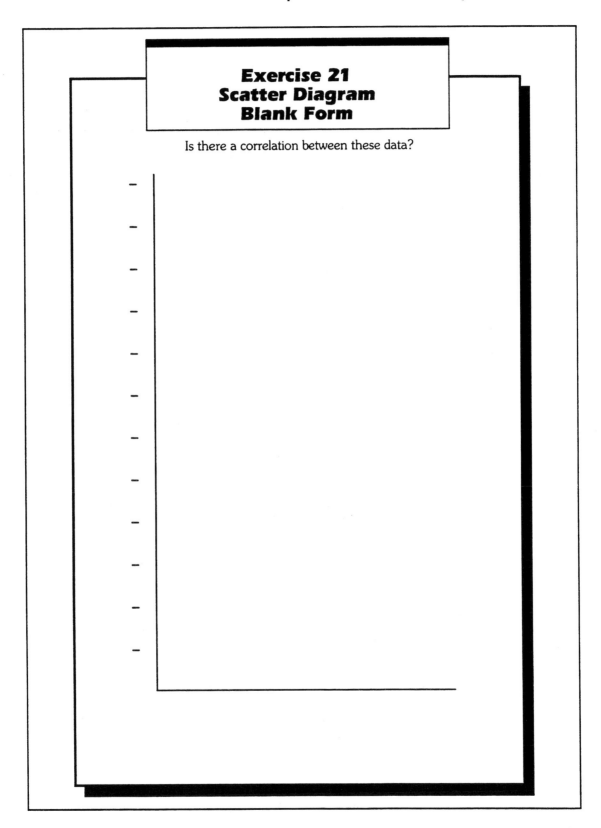

Exercise 21
Data for Scatter Diagram
Apex Hotel, 1989-1991

Month	Average Room Occupancy	Pounds of Linen per Day	
January	219	2284	**1989**
February	213	2916	
March	205	2793	
April	242	3038	
May	244	3269	
June	229	3212	
July	225	2979	
August	220	3047	
September	221	3204	
October	198	2832	
November	207	3047	
December	217	2870	
January	221	2486	**1990**
February	211	2828	
March	195	2525	
April	250	3081	
May	231	2895	
June	216	2818	
July	209	2800	
August	202	2756	
September	207	2945	
October	191	2706	
November	218	3072	
December	207	2592	
January	219	2848	**1991**
February	224	2883	
March	202	2680	
April	218	2846	
May	218	3357	
June	210	2558	
July	217	2821	
August	204	2588	
September	205	2945	
October	199	2819	
November	173	2708	
December	187	2474	

NOTES

Exercise 22 Instructions

A Snapshot of the Big Picture: Bar Graphs and Pie Charts

Purpose

The purpose of this exercise is to introduce the bar graph and the pie chart to problem-solving teams. These tools are most effective if introduced to the team on an as-needed basis. For details on how to construct these tools, please reference *The Memory Jogger*™ or *A Guide to Graphical Problem Solving Processes*.

Preparation

- ○ Give each participant a copy of the exercise.
- ○ Provide enough pens and pencils for everyone.
- ○ Lay out several multicolored felt tip markers for anyone to use.
- ○ Set up a flip chart or writing board in the area.

Process

- ○ Explain to participants how to construct the bar graph and the pie chart.
- ○ Give each participant a copy of the bar graph/pie chart data, and a copy of "bar graph/pie chart, blank form."
- ○ Ask participants to complete the bar graph and pie chart.

Discussion

- ○ Ask participants to describe what information they can derive from these charts. (Two different ways to describe data.)
- ○ Ask participants to describe possible uses for this tool in their process.
- ○ Ask participants to describe the learnings they have derived from this tool.

▶ Time required: 15–30 minutes total
▶ Group size: Optimum is 4–9 people, but up to 20 people is acceptable

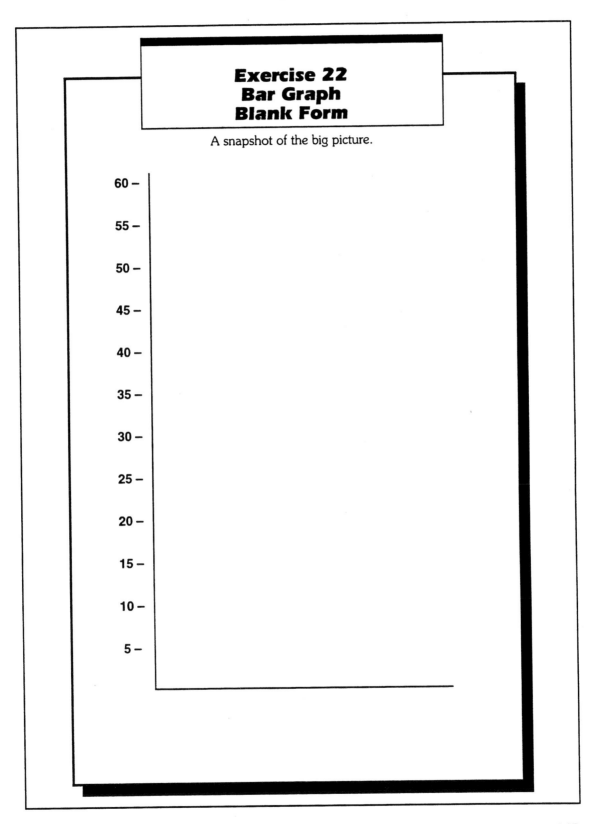

Exercise 22
Bar Graph
Blank Form

A snapshot of the big picture.

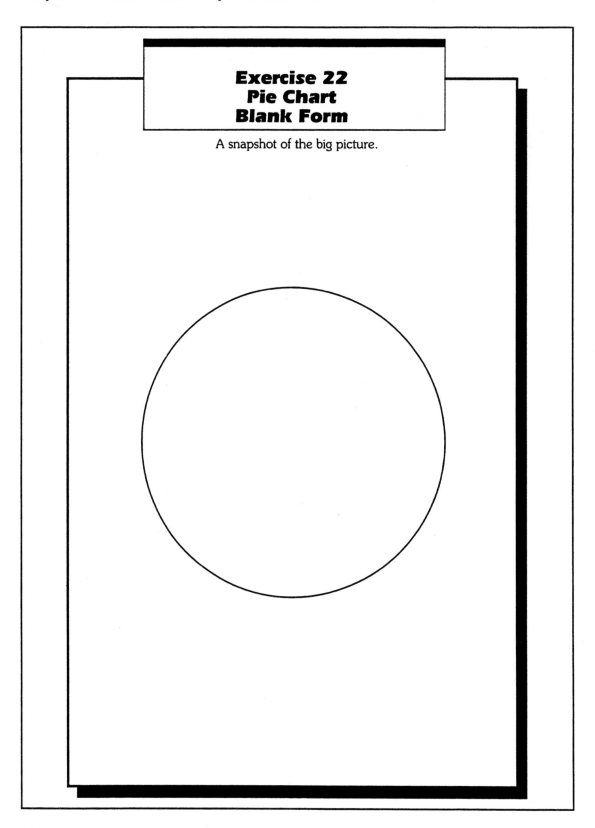

**Exercise 22
Pie Chart
Blank Form**

A snapshot of the big picture.

Exercise 22
Data for Bar Graph
and Pie Chart

Ace Package Delivery

The following data was collected on
customer complaints in April

Package Delivered

Late	22%
Damaged	12%
Wrong Address	37%
Other	29%

Exercise 23 Instructions

Back to the Root: Solution & Effect Diagrams

Purpose

The purpose of this exercise is to introduce the solution & effect diagram to problem-solving teams. This tool is most effective if introduced to the team on an as-needed basis. For details on how to construct this tool, see the section in this chapter called "Step 10: Generate Solutions."

Preparation

- ○ Give each participant a copy of the exercise.
- ○ Provide enough pens and pencils for everyone.
- ○ Lay out several multicolored felt tip markers for anyone to use.
- ○ Set up a flip chart or writing board in the area.

Process

- ○ Explain to participants how to construct the solution & effect diagram.
- ○ Ask participants to complete the diagram.

Discussion

- ○ Ask participants to describe what information they can derive from this diagram.
- ○ Ask participants to describe possible uses for this tool in their process.
- ○ Ask participants to describe the learnings they have derived from this tool.

- ▶ Time required: 30–45 minutes total
- ▶ Group size: Optimum is 4–9 people, but up to 20 people is acceptable

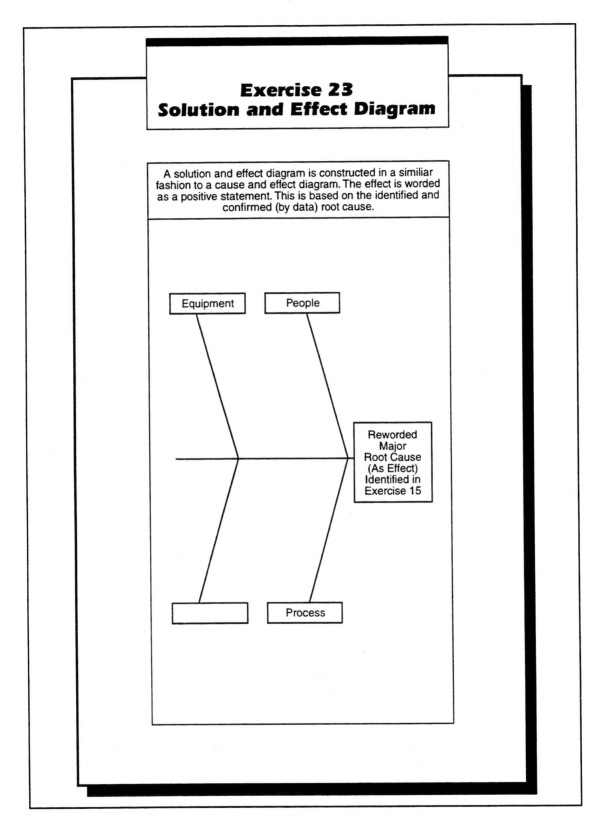

Exercise 23
Solution and Effect Diagram

A solution and effect diagram is constructed in a similiar fashion to a cause and effect diagram. The effect is worded as a positive statement. This is based on the identified and confirmed (by data) root cause.

Equipment

People

Reworded Major Root Cause (As Effect) Identified in Exercise 15

Process

Exercise 24 Instructions

What is Driving Us to Use Teams? Force Field Diagrams

Purpose

The purpose of this exercise is to introduce the force field diagram to problem-solving teams. This tool is most effective if introduced to the team on an as-needed basis. For details on how to construct this tool, please reference *The Memory Jogger*™, *The Memory Jogger*™ *II*, or *A Guide to Graphical Problem Solving Processes*. For details on how to facilitate the construction and use of this tool, reference the *Coach's Guide to The Memory Jogger*™ *II*.

Preparation

- ◌ Give each participant a copy of the exercise.
- ◌ Provide enough pens and pencils for everyone.
- ◌ Lay out several multicolored felt tip markers for anyone to use.
- ◌ Set up a flip chart or writing board in the area.

Process

- ◌ Explain to participants how to construct the force field diagram.
- ◌ Ask participants to complete the force field diagram on "What is driving us to use teams?"

Discussion

- ◌ Ask participants to describe what information they can derive from this chart.
- ◌ Ask participants to describe possible uses for this tool in their process.
- ◌ Ask participants to describe the learnings they have derived from this tool.

- ▶ Time required: 30–45 minutes total
- ▶ Group size: Optimum is 4–9 people, but up to 20 people is acceptable

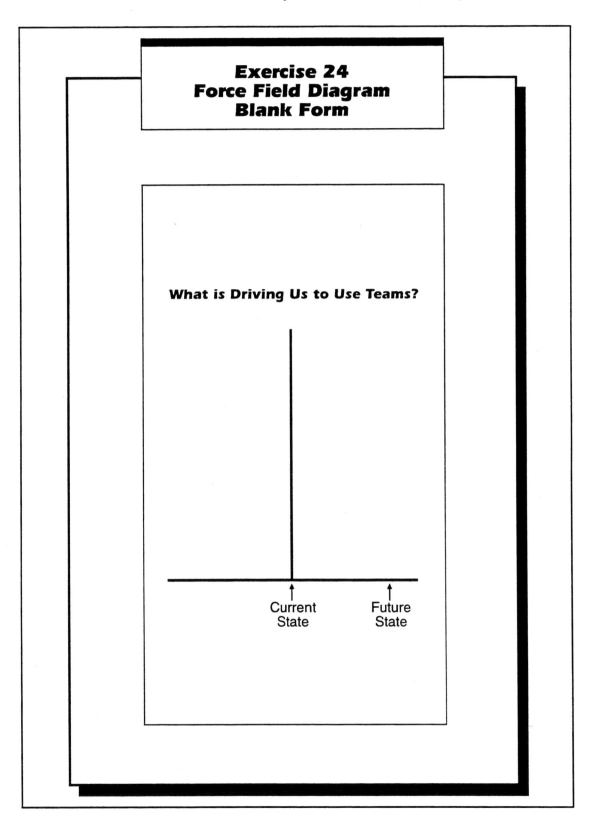

**Exercise 24
Force Field Diagram
Blank Form**

What is Driving Us to Use Teams?

Current
State

Future
State

NOTES

Chapter 9
Rewards and Recognition

Key Points

- How should organizations reward change? Initiative? Teamwork?
- Give recognition to people, not the reward system
- Some examples of how to reward people
- Do team-oriented companies reward individual efforts?
- Some possible approaches to rewarding people as teams

Rewards and recognition is a phrase that you often hear in discussions about teams and when an organization is attempting to change its culture to reflect its interpretation of how the organization is implementing TQM. Many of the issues today involve rewards and recognition, and many organizations struggle with knowing how to compensate positive team behavior. Unfortunately, traditional methods that did not work well for individuals are frequently used on teams

How Will Your Organization Reward Culture Change?

Culture change is very time consuming and expensive for an organization. In *Corporate Cultures*, (Addison-Wesley Publishing, 1992), the authors Terrence Deal and Allan Kennedy state that "To achieve even half of the change a company attempts, it must spend an amount equivalent to between 5 and 10 percent of its annual budget for the personnel whose behavior is supposed to be changed. Change is even more expensive to achieve than we had imagined! In other words, to get people in a culture to even begin to change, management has to capture 5 to 10 percent of their time for a year!" They also state that this change will not be successful if it is not lead from the top. To augment this top-down leadership, a formal system of rewarding and recognizing people is helpful.

Rewards and recognition by themselves cannot change a culture. People in an organization who are consistently rewarded and recognized for their good efforts to change old habits or think in new ways, however, *can and will* influence other people's attitudes and behavior in the process of a culture change. Because of this correlation of the reward system to the desired culture, it is essential that organizations integrate the reward system with the culture change process. The team culture is foreign to how many organizations have done business in the past, therefore each organization will have to develop a reward structure consistent with its new culture but within the context of its current culture. When organizations emphasize short-term rewards, such as giving team members prime parking places for a job well done, they shortchange their employees of the true recognition they deserve. Short-term rewards do little to motivate people to work together and destroy people's confidence in themselves as valuable contributors when the rewards are inconsistent.

Some organizations have in place a system of rewards that compensates individuals by bestowing them with special privileges. For example, a particular pay level or type of position may warrant a certain size or location office. Some organizations grant reserved parking places, exclusive-use badges, or other types of individual recognition for specific accomplishments or a promotion to a specific job title or function. These type of rewards do more to destroy a team culture than to build one.

In an organization that is changing its culture by taking a growing teams approach, many of the traditional rewards will need to be abandoned and new, more appropriate rewards developed. Top management needs to regard the reward system as worthwhile. The entire organization will need to be trained to recognize the worth of these rewards and the desire to receive these new rewards must supplant the desire to receive the old rewards. In today's work environment, adequate compensation, responsibility, accountability and trust are needed to buoy the workforce. Basing rewards and recognition on these needs should become the basis for team compensation systems.

The old reward structure should be dismantled. This will not be easy and will take time and resources that must be included in the plan for growing the team culture. Small companies are leading the way in this vital area, since their culture, while often just as ingrained, can be changed more quickly because fewer people are required to adapt to the new culture.

Is Your Organization Rewarding People or Systems?

Whenever the subject of rewards and recognition comes up, employees will want to know how much more money they will receive in their paychecks, and management will want to know how much more the reward system will cost. In reality, most of the reward and recognition methods that have proven successful have resulted in very little additional costs, and the value added by the teams offset these costs.

Some of the more familiar rewards that come to many peoples' minds are traditional and inexpensive, such as bringing in food and drinks for teams. (For example, coffee and donuts, pizza and beer.) If appropriately timed, these kinds of bonuses can provide short-term incentives to some team members, and if acknowledged as an important bonus to the new culture, can provide an avenue for others to participate.

Some organizations have developed a "team success display wall." The teams' projects and their results are posted. Success is based on how well the teams met the success criteria they developed. Some teams are ongoing, so their success criteria will be different, but it is still important that their successful efforts be recognized. One pitfall of posting the results of team projects is that this type of recognition may become a team objective, and not a team's criteria for success. Many employees are just happy to have the chance to participate, help make decisions, and see these decisions implemented.

Some organizations have evolved in different directions and the rewards they have developed appear to have a lasting impact in changing the *system* that rewards people. These changes were driven from the top down and specific actions were rewarded. The people in these organizations were trained to work in different ways and to respond to different reward stimuli.

Some Examples of How Organizations Can Reward People

One example of an organization's reward system is a team we observed that was responsible for developing an appropriate system for rewards and recognition. This team developed a team-driven performance system for management. The system was on-line for anyone to access. Team goals were entered into the system, as well as the team's measurables, actions the team was taking, and daily progress. Making this information visible to each team member and other teams increased interaction between people and more information was shared. Goal attainment is now at 99 percent on a weekly basis, and recognition by all members of the company is immediate.

In another organization that has spent several years growing a team culture, one layer of management was eliminated. (The managers who wanted to stay were retained in different positions, most of them in the direct workforce in the new team culture.) The teams then received the bonuses that this layer of management normally received based on overall performance of the company.

In another organization that was trying to empower employees, they found that many employees at first resisted this change in culture. As with many people, the employees felt comfortable in the old ways of doing business and resisted the organization's new push to empower them. Even the bold ones who were willing to try this "empowerment stuff" were very cautious and tried to work within the existing system. To overcome this cautiousness, senior management developed several different types of rewards that the CEO pressented at meetings held during working hours. Everyone in the plant is asked to attend these ceremonies. One of the rewards is the "All-Star Award," which is given to the people who take the initiative to resolve customer and cost-related issues. Another award is the "Walking Shoes Award," which is given to the people who take a big step toward empowerment and show success through innovation or risk taking. All of this organization's awards also come with a point value that can be redeemed for goods that are valuable to the recipients.

One government organization that has been growing a team culture for over six years has developed, what for them is, a very significant reward system. Teams get to make a presentation to the base commander and his top staff of what they are working on, what they have accomplished, and their targets. While this may not seem like a reward to some, in this environment, where most of the team members have never seen or dealt with the top levels, it is a very energizing experience. These team members are all trained in presentation techniques to help them overcome their fears, and to receive training in good practices of teamwork, the roles and responsibilities of team members, and the functions of teams.

Team reviews take place both in the commander's office and at the team member's work areas. At the commander's insistence, teams have been asked to present the actual charts and graphs that they used at team meetings. The commander's focus is on results, not presentations. These presentations are now seen as a reward for a job well done, although at the beginning of the team growing process, many people felt that this presentation was a threat to show their failures in the new culture.

Another type of reward that team members may perceive as such is public communication of team successes and team project "flukes." One large company in California has a newsletter dedicated to team projects. This newsletter contains numerous stories of successes and failures and often results in reducing duplication of effort since no one in the organization knows how many teams are functioning or what they are working on. This company's concern is that the team culture is working. It is not concerned with keeping count of the number of teams, the number of participants, and the number of problems they are working on.

Do Team Cultures Reward the Individual or the Team?

Most organizations that have decided to change to a team culture soon run into the problem of how to give individuals performance reviews when they are working within a team structure. Team members are very interested in ensuring that their paychecks are not affected by the new team structure.

There are several approaches that have been tried and many more we think that will be developed in the future. One approach is to develop a team-based reward structure. The team is reviewed as a unit based on their performance to goals and agreed upon measurements. All members of the team receive an equal percentage at review time. Another approach to compensation is to pay individuals for the skills they possess. Each person in this type of system learns as many job functions on the team as possible through training and on-the-job learning. When someone shows competence in each area, that person becomes a more valuable member of the team and is rewarded accordingly. Often, the team itself provides the criteria and evaluation of its members and is responsible for distributing the percentages based on these criteria. One last approach is to tie team compensation directly to the performance of the organization. As the organization makes more money, teams are rewarded.

Some Possible Approaches to Rewarding People as Teams

We have examined a number of potentially useful team compensation systems. One of the more intriguing models is that proposed by Norman W. Young. He has proposed the following team-based compensation model:

> In virtually any book or article on quality or teams, one will find a discussion on reward and recognition. In this discussion will come the sage wisdom that incentives should be focused on the success of the team rather than on superior individual performance. Great! We all agree. Now let's get off the discussion of how to reformat the employee of the month award to make it a team of the month award, and talk about the base issue, compensation. For whatever other reasons we get up and go to work, there is one underlying reason, and that is money. In this modern world of credits and debts, making money is the equivalent of waking up and leaving the cave with a club to "kill something to eat." There are only two rules. The first, "No kill, no eat" and the second, "Don't get killed by your lunch." Take away the money and most of us would at very least change jobs.
>
> This model is based on a company which sells a product and in return receives revenue from a customer. The company is composed of a number of teams which perform functions in the process of creating (including conceiving, designing, delivering, and servicing) the product. Each team is made up of individuals of varying experience, with varying skills and education. The compensation plan proposed is designed to be changed by any entity that adopts it BUT the driving principles are not.
>
> **Principle 1:**
> Over the long term, a company cannot pay more for functions than it receives in revenue. (A balanced budget is mandatory. You can't eat air.)
>
> Principle 2:
> The company must compensate teams, not individuals. (This is the only way to ultimately

encourage working together. The hunter that didn't get any of the meat, killed the other hunters.)

Principle 3:
There must be opportunity for each person to affect and improve their own compensation by adding value to the team. (This insures personal incentive and participation.)
First, it is the responsibility of the company to set the value of its product(s) at a fair market rate so that they can be sold and yield an acceptable profit. Ideally this is done by a team which includes market analysis skills, a broad knowledge of the components of product cost, and representatives of all areas that have direct customer contact (sales, service, billing, etc.). It is this revenue which provides the source of all compensation to the teams, and therefore the team compensation MUST come back to this basis in order for teams to see and feel the relationship between their efforts and customer needs. Team earnings should not increase if company revenue is falling (and this includes the management and executive teams).

A recommended method for implementing the distribution of revenue to the teams is to establish "customer satisfaction credits" (CSCs). With a representative of each team, develop a list of those functions that contribute to meeting the needs of the customer. Using a "forced choice matrix" in combination with the nominal group technique (authors' note: other tools will work equally well), rank the items from top to bottom and assign CSCs as appropriate. Armed with a list which is in essence a joint agreement on how to meet the needs of the customer, CSCs are given to each team based on the list. Clearly this is a tremendous task in a large company, but it can be facilitated by working at the smallest segment of the organization for which clear revenue and contributions can be defined.

At this point it is possible to determine the dollar value of each team's compensation as follows:

Team Compensation = Unit Revenue X (Team CSCs/Unit CSCs)

Individual compensation within the team is determined by the team using a system of team value credits (TVCs). Again using appropriate tools, the members of the team determine the things which they value within their team and develop a system of credits for each. Some of these credits might be:

- Formal education (different credits for different levels)
- Industry training
- Job experience
- Special skills (SPC, public speaking, etcetera.)
- Years of service within the team
- Number of different team jobs that a person can perform
- Extra training
- Extra time spent to help the team succeed

Once credits are assigned to this list, and each team member is evaluated BY THE TEAM, it is possible to determine the dollar value of each team member's compensation as follows:

Individual Compensation = Team Revenue X (member's TVCs/Team CSCs)

As an aside, lest we totally skirt the issue of individual recognition, individual recognition should come from within the team. The members of the team are the ones who are most likely to see openly the actual contribution of an individual to the team. Often the most valuable recognition is the respect afforded on a day-to-day basis. There may also be times that the team wants to express recognition in a more tangible manner. When this happens, it should clearly be a consensus expression, receiving approval of all members of the team. One way to do this in the context of the model is to grant recognition credits for a fixed period of time. These can be drawn from a pool, which has been set aside in advance, or by the direct yielding of individual credits by all other members of the team. This is a transaction that should take place within the team at the team's discretion. Those outside the team should not see or participate in this event.

A further note is that the same system might be used to define and evaluate candidates for addition to the team. If each candidate is assigned credits using the system, then it is a relatively simple matter to select the candidate who most closely matches the credit list of the position to be filled. Compensation is clearly determined in advance and further negotiation is not necessary.

— Norman W. Young

Whatever compensation system organizations develop must be consistent with the new cultural rewards they wish to become the standard for their organizations. Rewards and recognition are not enough to change the culture of an organization, however, they can be valuable to the organization in beginning and continuing this change.

Exercise 25 Instructions

How Do You Reward and Recognize Team Efforts?

Purpose

For team growth to continue, rewards and recognition must be considered for all members on a continual basis. This exercise lists fourteen specific examples of how the members of your team may wish to be recognized.

Preparation

- Give each participant a copy of the exercise.
- Provide enough pens and pencils for everyone.
- Lay out multicolored felt tip markers for anyone to use.
- Set up a flip chart or writing board in the area.

Process

- Ask participants to review the list and circle five ideas that they think might have a positive impact on their team.
- Ask participants to add at least one more idea for number 15. Additional ideas are welcome.
- Allow five minutes for participants to complete this exercise.

Discussion

- Review each idea, beginning with number 1.
- Query participants for, both pro and con, comments on each idea and write some brief remarks on a flip chart or board.
- Ask participants to take notes on how they might use any of the ideas for their team.
- On a separate sheet of flip chart paper, write down the ideas given for number 15. As each idea is presented, discuss it briefly. Participants may think of more ideas!

► Time required: 60–90 minutes total
► Group size: Optimum is 4–9, but up to 20 people is acceptable

Exercise 25
How Do You Reward and Recognize Team Efforts?

Time: 5 minutes

Some ideas for discussion.

Recognition is important to all of us, and while people in organizations may often recognize individuals for their accomplishments, it is just as important to recognize teams when their performance is successful.

Some forms of rewards and recognition are listed below. Which ones would have the greatest positive impact on your team? Why? Pick five from the list, then add at least one more idea for recognizing team accomplishments.

1   A personal gift for each member

2   A presentation of results to management

3   An opportunity to work for a limited time in another area, building, or location

4   Competition with other teams with results displayed

5   A presentation of results to co-workers

6   Publicity in the organization's internal newsletter

7   Positive critique of technical content and presentation method by management

8   An opportunity to visit another organization or a trip to a supplier's facility

9   A party or group celebration

10   Publicity in the local newspaper

11   A videotape for each member from the team's celebration

12   A charitable contribution made by the company in the team's name

13   A plaque prominently displayed that recognizes the team or a team idea

14   Enable as many members as possible to be involved in the installation and start-up phase of implementing a team idea

15   _____

NOTES

Chapter 10
Growth and Change: A Summary

As organizations grow and adapt to a team culture, their ability to respond to the needs of their customers is broadened and response significantly improves. The most visible change is a consistent focus on the Plan, Do, Check, and Act (PDCA) cycle and the Standardize, Do, Check, and Act (SDCA) cycle. In addition, all individuals in an organization develop the ability to clearly identify their customers, their critical processes, their measures of success, and understand how they are linked to the organization's vision and mission.

Use of the PDCA cycle on a continual basis is a developmental process that should be encouraged by each team member at every opportunity. Its integration becomes complete when individuals no longer separate their work into "TQM work" and their "real work."

As an organization's culture changes and initial teams are nurtured into high-performance teams, the role of management changes to one of leadership. Direct supervision takes on a much lesser role—supervisors work instead to remove barriers and align the vision of the organization with the needs of the organization's customers. As teams develop further, many of the traditional middle management and supervisory positions may disappear altogether and these people's talents can be used in different ways to better meet the needs of customers and the organization.

Teams must not be started and left to fend for themselves. If teams are worth beginning, they are worth nurturing and carefully developing. This takes a real commitment from management and a conscious effort on the part of all of those who are involved.

The benefits of teams can be tremendous with total commitment from top management, however, starting teams without this commitment is an open invitation to disaster. Many organizations feel that their commitment is best shown by keeping score as to the number of teams, number of participants, and so forth. What these organizations are really doing is not committing to the cultural change, rather, they are trying to maintain the status quo while fooling themselves into believing that starting teams will accomplish their goals.

Organizations must realize that culture change is neither easy nor inexpensive. People do not change easily. They must be led. This leadership must come from the very top levels of the organization and must be consistent and continual.

Organizations that have managed this cultural change have had significant, measurable results in the morale of their employees, and have increased their customers' satisfaction, as indicated by increased sales. In addition, employees feel like they have been able to contribute and have a feeling of satisfaction because they have a direct impact on their customers.

This book has provided a roadmap for growing teams, based on our experience in growing and leading successful teams. This roadmap begins with an organization's commitment to culture change through the teaming process. By developing a team culture and gradually growing teams, the people in an organization are encouraged to express their ideas in a team. Processes are improved by the most knowledgeable individuals. This team nurturing initially provides a feeling of safety through numbers. A team presenting an improvement idea has more of an impact than an individual.

Growing teams requires organizations to focus on what they want to change. Change is usually met with resistance. One of the primary reasons for this resistance is that a habitual behavior is being attacked. Have you ever tried to stop smoking, drinking, or eating too much? The change is difficult. Culture change, as well, requires people to modify learned behaviors; behaviors that were once acceptable. Before organizations start to grow teams, they need to understand what team building is, who is involved, what process will be used, and why all employees would want to participate.

As teams continue to grow, management needs to continue its commitment to a team culture. It needs to nurture teams by coaching team members, allowing teams to grow through mistakes, and keeping communications open to enable team members to work together. Preventive maintenance is required to keep teams working effectively. In maintaining productive teams, some topics that should be addressed are: how to assess team progress, the positive attitudes of effective team builders and how actions will match attitudes, how to encourage optimum team member relationships and behaviors, how to focus consistently on the problem and not each other, and how to analyze the impact of teams on the organization.

When organizations start to grow teams, management should be savvy enough to expect resistance and plan how to work with it. One simple, conceptual way to work with resistance is to ask everyone to believe the organization's future depends on a culture change—from belief comes the commitment and actions to make change happen. This commitment must come from the top and be demonstrated on a consistent basis.

Nurturing teams takes place at all levels of the organization. It begins at the highest levels of the organization and encompass all aspects of the organization. Management can truly empower employees, and thus nurture teams, by asking people to get involved in the team process, allow teams to make changes and improvements to their processes, give teams permission to choose the areas they want to improve, give its support by publicly recognizing team accomplishments or defending team failures, establish parameters for team projects, and share the responsiblity of success and failure with team members.

Teams should follow a consistent process-improvement model that is based on the organization's culture. Measurements should be a consistent and integral part of the model.

Managers' roles and responsibilities in the team process are critical. Management is the key to making or breaking the team process. It is not what management says, but what it does that can nurture the growth of a team culture or slowly starve it.

Management needs to provide a supportive environment with high expectations for teams. Many managers are at first fearful of the team approach since they have been successful for a number of years demonstrating the very behaviors they are now having to change—such as fire fighting, working as individual contributors, and assuming 100 percent of the responsibility for projects that fail, as well as those that succeed.

Middle management needs to develop the functional activities to meet the organization's vision and mission, align the top executives' vision with the needs of the team's customers, and provide feedback to top executives based on the data developed by the teams. In addition, management's responsibilities include coordination of team activities, advice on issue selection, providing for needed resources, removal of barriers, assistance in implementation of solutions, and recognition of team achievement. Managers normally only participate on teams of managers. If they are involved with other teams, unintentional barriers are often raised. In addition, the presence of management often makes teams feel that they are not really trusted to make decisions.

The attitude of a team can be easily influenced by the actions team members observe in those above them, those who have participated on previous teams, and those participating on the same team. It is important that all members of the team feel their contributions have value and that they are being heard. Team leaders and facilitators must be especially careful to elicit a response from each team member for each decision that is reached. Voting is not sufficient, consensus is required. If consensus is not reached, future decisions and actions by the team may become meaningless. No matter how often voting is done, or how strong the vote, it can never make a wrong right and it can never change the mind of an individual. Teams should be rewarded for their acceptance of this culture change.

Rewards and recognition in themselves cannot change a culture, however, they can influence a culture change. Because of this correlation of the reward to the desired culture, it is imperative that organizations integrate their rewards with the culture change process. The team culture is foreign to how we have done business in the past, therefore each organization will have to develop a reward structure consistent with its new culture but within the context of its current culture.

Throughout the book, we have provided exercises that can help organizations in their culture change journey. These exercises have been very helpful in numerous organizations and are often modified to fit an organization's culture. We have provided a roadmap for the journey to growing teams. Just like any roadmap, there are many routes that lead to the same place. Some are more direct. Some are more easily traveled than others. The key is that you, as an organization, know from where you want to begin, where you want to go, and what you want to measure to evaluate your success in getting there.

The culture change to growing teams requires significant time, effort, and resources and should not be undertaken without a thorough understanding and deep commitment at the top levels of the organization.

This page is intentionally left blank.

Exercises 26-29 Instructions

Keep the Focus: Analyze Your Team's Process

Purpose

After organizations have begun the teaming process, they need to review the effectiveness of the process. Exercise 2 focused the organization on effective qualities required for beginning teams. This exercise is the audit of that process, helping to analyze the team process as it has developed.

Preparation

- ○   Give each participant a copy of the exercise.
- ○   Provide enough pens and pencils for everyone.
- ○   Lay out multicolored felt tip markers for anyone to use.
- ○   Set up a flip chart or writing board in the area.

Process

- ○   Ask participants to score all of the statements in the following four exercises.
- ○   The four possible responses are agree, disagree, strongly agree, or strongly disagree.
- ○   Allow 12 minutes for participants to complete all four exercises.
- ○   Teams should be brought to consensus on each statement.
- ○   Plot the consensus results on a radar chart. (See example of a radar chart in Chapter 1.)

Discussion

- ○   Work to reach consensus on each statement.
- ○   The facilitator should capture the reasons why each particular consensus score was agreed to.

    Time required: 60–75 minutes total
    Group size: Optimum is 4–9 people, but up to 20 people is acceptable

Consensus

Each person can live with a decision,
but may not feel it is the *best* decision.

Exercise 26
Time: 2 minutes
Keep the Focus: Analyze Your Team's Process
Quality Improvement Culture

1 Management trusts the quality improvement teams to do their work without controlled supervision.

❏ Strongly Disagree   ❏ Disagree   ❏ Agree   ❏ Strongly Agree

2 It is our job to improve our work process continuously.

❏ Strongly Disagree   ❏ Disagree   ❏ Agree   ❏ Strongly Agree

3 We know senior management's vision for the future and know how our improvement efforts fit this vision.

❏ Strongly Disagree   ❏ Disagree   ❏ Agree   ❏ Strongly Agree

4 The vision for our future is exciting.

❏ Strongly Disagree   ❏ Disagree   ❏ Agree   ❏ Strongly Agree

5 I feel that these quality improvement teams are worthwhile.

❏ Strongly Disagree   ❏ Disagree   ❏ Agree   ❏ Strongly Agree

6 When team solutions are instituted, the organization makes a real effort to hold the gain.

❏ Strongly Disagree   ❏ Disagree   ❏ Agree   ❏ Strongly Agree

Exercise 27
Time: 2 minutes
Keep the Focus: Analyze Your Team's Process
Team Meetings

1 Agendas were set up before the meetings, and everyone was clear on what was to be achieved.

❒ Strongly Disagree   ❒ Disagree   ❒ Agree   ❒ Strongly Agree

2 After each meeting, we all clearly understand what was discussed and/or agreed to.

❒ Strongly Disagree   ❒ Disagree   ❒ Agree   ❒ Strongly Agree

3 Group discussions are orderly and ideas seldom get lost.

❒ Strongly Disagree   ❒ Disagree   ❒ Agree   ❒ Strongly Agree

4 Everyone in the group takes an active part in the discussion.

❒ Strongly Disagree   ❒ Disagree   ❒ Agree   ❒ Strongly Agree

5 Group discussions are not dominated by a few individuals.

❒ Strongly Disagree   ❒ Disagree   ❒ Agree   ❒ Strongly Agree

6 We disagree in an orderly manner without causing defensive reactions.

❒ Strongly Disagree   ❒ Disagree   ❒ Agree   ❒ Strongly Agree

7 Team members trust and respect each other.

❒ Strongly Disagree   ❒ Disagree   ❒ Agree   ❒ Strongly Agree

8 Team members are sensitive to the needs and concerns of each other.

❒ Strongly Disagree   ❒ Disagree   ❒ Agree   ❒ Strongly Agree

Exercise 28
Time: 4 minutes

Keep the Focus: Analyze Your Team's Process

Team Problem Solving

1 The team carefully diagnoses problems before solutions are proposed (there is a methodology).

❏ Strongly Disagree   ❏ Disagree   ❏ Agree   ❏ Strongly Agree

2 Decisions are made by consensus and team members support the decisions.

❏ Strongly Disagree   ❏ Disagree   ❏ Agree   ❏ Strongly Agree

3 Each team member has had the appropriate training to function effectively on the team.

❏ Strongly Disagree   ❏ Disagree   ❏ Agree   ❏ Strongly Agree

4 Our team problem solving is customer focused.

❏ Strongly Disagree   ❏ Disagree   ❏ Agree   ❏ Strongly Agree

5 There is a "team spirit" of mutual helpfulness and shared ownership within our team.

❏ Strongly Disagree   ❏ Disagree   ❏ Agree   ❏ Strongly Agree

6 Our facilitators are helpful and additive to our problem-solving process.

❏ Strongly Disagree   ❏ Disagree   ❏ Agree   ❏ Strongly Agree

7 Our team develops specific action plans of what, when, and by whom an action will be taken.

❏ Strongly Disagree   ❏ Disagree   ❏ Agree   ❏ Strongly Agree

8 We celebrate the success of our team.

❏ Strongly Disagree   ❏ Disagree   ❏ Agree   ❏ Strongly Agree

9 Management respects our decisions and helps us to implement our solutions.

❏ Strongly Disagree   ❏ Disagree   ❏ Agree   ❏ Strongly Agree

10 We receive the necessary outside support or expertise when our team needs it.

❏ Strongly Disagree   ❏ Disagree   ❏ Agree   ❏ Strongly Agree

11 When our solutions are implemented, they make a difference and the organization experiences real gains.

❏ Strongly Disagree   ❏ Disagree   ❏ Agree   ❏ Strongly Agree

Exercise 29
Time: 4 minutes
Keep the Focus: Analyze Your Team's Process
High-Performance Teams

1 Team members share a sense of purpose and are clear about what the team intends to achieve.

 ❑ Strongly Disagree   ❑ Disagree   ❑ Agree   ❑ Strongly Agree

2 Members are confident about the team's ability to overcome obstacles and realize its vision.

 ❑ Strongly Disagree   ❑ Disagree   ❑ Agree   ❑ Strongly Agree

3 Each person feels pride in being a member of the team.

 ❑ Strongly Disagree   ❑ Disagree   ❑ Agree   ❑ Strongly Agree

4 Members are enthusiastic about the work of the team.

 ❑ Strongly Disagree   ❑ Disagree   ❑ Agree   ❑ Strongly Agree

5 Recognition of individual and team accomplishments is provided regularly.

 ❑ Strongly Disagree   ❑ Disagree   ❑ Agree   ❑ Strongly Agree

6 Members are committed to high standards and quality results.

 ❑ Strongly Disagree   ❑ Disagree   ❑ Agree   ❑ Strongly Agree

7 All members have developed strong skills in the team process.

 ❑ Strongly Disagree   ❑ Disagree   ❑ Agree   ❑ Strongly Agree

8 Members demonstrate flexibility and perform whatever task and/or maintenance function is required.

 ❑ Strongly Disagree   ❑ Disagree   ❑ Agree   ❑ Strongly Agree

9 The team has a reputation for being open to both opinions and feelings, hard work, and fun.

 ❑ Strongly Disagree   ❑ Disagree   ❑ Agree   ❑ Strongly Agree

10 Members are committed to open communication and believe they can state their opinions, thoughts, and feelings without fear.

 ❑ Strongly Disagree   ❑ Disagree   ❑ Agree   ❑ Strongly Agree

11 Through honest, empathetic feedback, members are made aware of their strengths and weaknesses as team members.

 ❑ Strongly Disagree   ❑ Disagree   ❑ Agree   ❑ Strongly Agree

12 Opportunities to grow and learn new skills are provided regularly.

 ❑ Strongly Disagree   ❑ Disagree   ❑ Agree   ❑ Strongly Agree

Appendix A

Herrmann Brain Dominance Profile

The following description is an excerpted version of an article "The Whole-Brain Affinity Model: A Synthesized Approach to Surfacing Creative Concepts," written by Glen Hoffherr, John Moran, and Richard Talbot. The article appeared in GOAL/QPC's Competitive Times™ newsletter, issue 3, 1991.

The Herrmann Brain Dominance Model was developed by Ned Herrmann in 1975 as a metaphorical interpretation of how we think and what our preferred modes of knowing are. The model is a synthesis of the research of Roger Sperry and Paul MacLean. Sperry, who is a Nobel Prize recipient, and his associates did much of the testing that validated the specialization of the brain's hemispheres. MacLean developed the evolutionary concept of brain development: the triune brain. Herrmann combined both concepts to build a thinking styles model.

The Herrmann Brain Dominance model contains four distinct thinking styles, those incorporating the left and right hemispheres, as well as those incorporating the upper (cerebral) and lower (limbic) parts of the brain. Thinking processes can therefore be described as upper (cerebral) left, lower (limbic) left, upper (cerebral) right, and lower (limbic) right. To facilitate your understanding, these four thinking processes will be referenced n the following way: upper left = A; lower left = B; lower right = C; upper right = D. The four quadrants are often color coded A-Blue, B-Green, C-Red, and D-Yellow. The metaphoric model is referenced as though one were looking at the back of a person's head.

The upper left "A" model of thinking can be thought of as analytical, mathematical, and technical. The lower left "B" can be thought of as controlled, conservative, organized, and administrative in nature. Lower right "C" thought is interpersonal, emotional, musical, and spiritual. Upper right "D" contains the imaginative, synthesizing, artistic, holistic, and conceptual modes. The whole-brain model is illustrated in the figure titled "Whole-Brain Model."

Herrmann Brain Dominance Profile

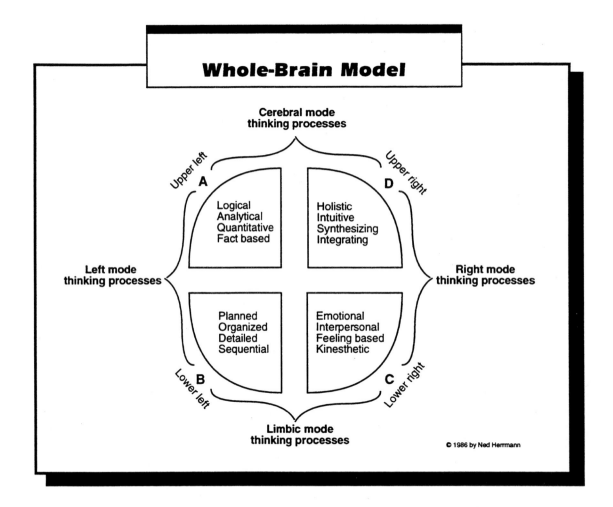

Herrmann Brain Dominance Profile

The figure below, "The 4 F's," illustrates the four different modes of thinking in abbreviated form: A-Facts, B-Form, C-Feelings, and D-Futures.

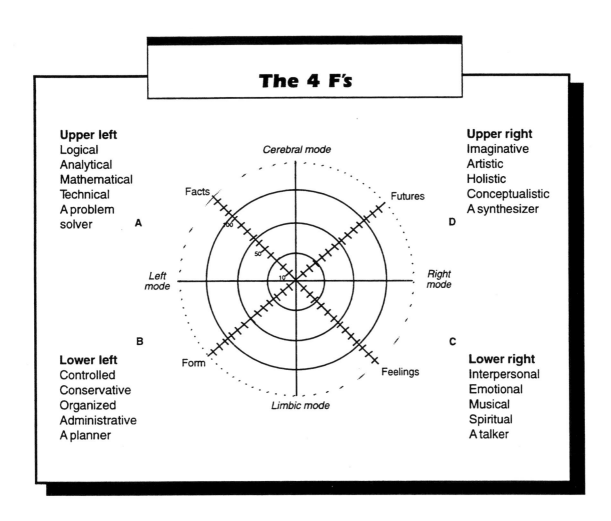

The 4 F's

Upper left
Logical
Analytical
Mathematical
Technical
A problem
solver

Upper right
Imaginative
Artistic
Holistic
Conceptualistic
A synthesizer

Cerebral mode

Facts

Futures

Left mode

Right mode

Limbic mode

Form

Feelings

Lower left
Controlled
Conservative
Organized
Administrative
A planner

Lower right
Interpersonal
Emotional
Musical
Spiritual
A talker

Meyers-Briggs Type Indicator

The Myers-Briggs Type Indicator (MBTI) is based on years of observing people by the psychologist Carl Jung and by the authors of the MBTI, Isabel Briggs Myers and her mother Katharine Cook Briggs. Their ideas help explain why different kinds of people are interested in different things, are good in different kinds of work, and often find it hard to understand each other. The Indicator was developed with great care and has been used with people around the world for more than twenty years. Families use it to understand each other better. Teachers and students use it to make learning more interesting and efficient. Young people and adults use it to choose careers that are likely to hold their interest and use their gifts. Organizations use the ideas of type to improve communication, teamwork, and leadership.

The MBTI assumes that every person uses eight of the qualities described by the letters "E" or "I," "S" or "N," "T" or "F," and "J" or "P," but that people find one letter of each pair more interesting or comfortable than its opposite. The letter "E" stands for extraversion, and "I" for introversion. The letter "S" for sensing, and "N" for intuition. The letter "T" stands for thinking, and "F" for feeling. The letter "J" stands for judgment, and "P" for perception.

To obtain more information on the Myers-Briggs Type Indicator, contact:

Consulting Psychologists Press, Inc.
3803 E. Bayshore Road
Palo Alto, California 94303

Another source of information is:

Center for Applications of Psychological Type
2720 N.W. 6th Street
Gainesville, Florida 32609

Selected Bibliography

Benson, Russell M., John W. Moran, and Richard P. Talbot. *A Guide to Graphical Problem-Solving Processes*. Milwaukee: ASQC Quality Press, 1990.

Brassard, Michael, and Diane Ritter. *The Memory Jogger™ II*. Methuen, MA: GOAL/QPC, 1994.

Brassard, Michael, ed. *The Memory Jogger™*. Methuen, MA: GOAL/QPC, 1988.

Brassard, Michael. *The Memory Jogger Plus+®*. Methuen, MA: GOAL/QPC, 1989.

Collett, Casey, Claudette Côté, and John W. Moran. *Daily Management: A System for Individual and Organizational Optimization*. Methuen, MA: GOAL/QPC, 1991.

Collett, Casey, Joseph Colletti, Joann DeMott, Glen D. Hoffherr, and John Moran. *Making Daily Management Work: A Perspective for Leaders and Managers*. Methuen, MA: GOAL/QPC, 1992.

GOAL/QPC. *Coach's Guide to The Memory Jogger™ II*. Methuen, MA: GOAL/QPC, 1995.

GOAL/QPC. *Voice of the Customer*. 1995 Research Report of the GOAL/QPC Research Committee. Methuen, MA: GOAL/QPC. 1995.

GOAL/QPC and Joiner Associates, Inc. *The Team Memory Jogger™*. Methuen, MA: GOAL/QPC, 1995.

Juran, J. M., Frank Gryna, eds. *Juran's Quality Control Handbook*, 4th ed. New York: McGraw-Hill Publishing Company, 1988.

About the Authors

Eugene C. Fetteroll Jr.
Mr. Fetteroll has more than 25 years of experience in all aspects of training for businesses ranging from manufacturing to service. He is a recipient of the Torch Award from the American Society for Training and Development. He helped produce *The Memory Jogger*™, published by GOAL/QPC.

Glen D. Hoffherr
Mr. Hoffherr has spent more than 20 years in management positions in high-technology industries. He has spoken at numerous conferences and consulted with more than 100 companies on different aspects of TQM implementation. Mr. Hoffherr is a coauthor of *Making Daily Management Work* and *Facilitating and Training in Quality Function Deployment.*

John W. Moran Jr., Ph.D.
Dr. Moran is a consultant who has provided management support to industry, government, health care, and service organizations in strategic planning, process optimization, and Total Quality Management (TQM). Dr. Moran has authored numerous articles, case studies, and textbooks in human relations, manufacturing management, statistics, operations research, materials management, Quality Function Deployment (QFD), and TQM.

GOAL/QPC Resources	Team Skills			
	Interpersonal Effectiveness	Data Collection and Analysis	Implementing Solutions	Managing Projects
Books				
The Memory Jogger™ II	●	●	●	●
The Team Memory Jogger™	●	●	●	●
The Memory Jogger™		●	●	
The Memory Jogger Plus+®			●	●
Coach's Guide to The Memory Jogger™ II	●	●	●	●
Power-Up Teams and Tools		●	●	
Problem-Solving Machine for The Memory Jogger™ II		●	●	
TQM: A Basic Text		●	●	●
Videos				
The Memory Jogger Plus+® Videotape Series			●	●
Integrated Management & Planning Tools: A Company Case Study			●	●
Basic Tools for Quality & Process Improvement Videotape Series		●	●	
Software				
The Memory Jogger™ Software (7 QC Tools)		●	●	
The Memory Jogger Plus+® Software (7 MP Tools)			●	●

To place an order or to inquire about our other products, call GOAL/QPC at 1-800-643-4316 or (603) 890-8800 Fax (603) 870-9122 Email at service@goalqpc.com, or find us on the Internet at http://www.goalqpc.com

Order Form

Code	Item Name/Title	Unit Price	Qty	Total

Subtotal	
Sales Tax Canada Only	
Shipping & Handling (see bottom of page)	
Total	

Payment Method (choose one)

❏ Check or Money Order attached $ _____
   (Make payable to GOAL/QPC)

❏ Purchase Order # _____
   (Attach a hard copy for all federal government orders)

❏ AMEX   ❏ Discover   ❏ Diners Club   ❏ MasterCard   ❏ VISA

Exp. Date: _____ / _____

Cardholder's Name _____
(please print)

Cardholder's Signature _____

Card Number

| | | | | | | | | | | | | | | | |
|1|2|3|4|5|6|7|8|9|10|11|12|13|14|15|16|

Payment Methods

We accept payment by check, money order, credit card, or purchase order. **If you are paying by purchase order:** 1) Provide the name and address of the person to be billed, or 2) Send a copy of the P.O. when order is payable by an agency of the federal government.

Bill To: (If different from "Ship To")

Name _____
Title _____
Company _____
Division/Dept. _____
Address _____
City _____ State/Province _____
Zip/Postal Code _____ Country _____
Phone _____ Fax _____
E-mail _____

Ship To: (Please use street address. We cannot ship to a P.O. Box.)

Name _____
Title _____
Company _____
Division/Dept. _____
Address _____
City _____ State/Province _____
Zip/Postal Code _____ Country _____
Phone _____ Fax _____
E-mail _____
GOAL/QPC Member Number _____
(needed for member discount)

☎ **Call Toll Free**
1-800-643-4316
(or 603-890-8800)
8:30 AM – 5:00 PM EST

✉ **Mail**
GOAL/QPC
2 Manor Parkway
Salem, NH 03079

✆ **Fax**
603-870-9122
Any Day, Any Time

Shipping & Handling
Continental US:
Orders up to $10 = $2 (US Mail). Orders $10 or more = $4 + 4% of the total order (guaranteed Ground Delivery). Call for Overnight, 2 & 3 day delivery. **For Alaska, Hawaii, Canada, Puerto Rico and other countries, please call.**

Sales Tax
Canada   7% of order

Visit our web site at www.goalqpc.com

Give Your Team the Edge it Needs to Succeed

The Team Memory Jogger™
A Pocket Guide for Team Members
A GOAL/QPC-Joiner Publication

Fits in your pocket

- Learn how to be an effective team member
- Identify key issues that your teams need to address
- Get work done more efficiently in teams
- Know when and how to end a project
- Manage conflict more effectively

The Team Memory Jogger™ is perfect for every member of your team. Each topic is discussed from the viewpoint of a team member and what one can contribute to the team. This friendly pocket guide is relevant to all kinds of teams; project, process improvement, self-directed or intact work teams, task forces and so on.

Written in collaboration with Joiner Associates, this new pocket guide has become a phenomenal hit for one simple reason—it contains teamwork strategies that really work. Since its introduction in 1995, many organizations have incorporated *The Team Memory Jogger™* as their standard reference in courses on team effectiveness.

The Team Memory Jogger™ goes beyond theory to provide you with practical, nuts-and-bolts action steps on how to be an effective team member. It is a perfect complement to *The Memory Jogger™ II*. Spiral-bound pocket guide measures 3.5" x 5.5". 1995. 164 pages. ISBN 1-879364-51-4. Code 1050E. $7.95 per copy. Quantity discounts available.

"Both The Team Memory Jogger™ and The Memory Jogger™ II
have played an important role in Inco's Ontario Division over the last six months.
We have included these pocket guides with our own training material for a
"Quality Overview" course, and attendees have said they are both
instructive and good references for facilitating groups, which they do
back in the workplace."

Bill Dopson,
Divisional TQ Coordinator,
Inco Limited (Ontario Division)

Everyone Contributes to Your ISO/QS 9000 Efforts

The Memory Jogger™ 9000

A Pocket Guide to Implementing the ISO 9000 Quality Systems Standard and QS-9000 Requirements

Robert Peach and Diane Ritter

Fits in your pocket

- Communicate the what, why, and how of ISO 9000
- Learn how to meet the ISO 9000 Standards and the QS-9000 Requirements
- Learn how to achieve and maintain ISO 9000/QS-9000 registration

The Memory Jogger™ 9000, an easy-to-use reference, is your everyday guide to the ISO 9000 Quality Systems Standards and QS-9000 Requirements. This is the first publication of its size to address a broad audience, not just the implementation team. It is packed with tips and potential pitfalls; flowcharts, figures, and checklists; documentation examples; definitions of key terms; and other illustrative and supplemental information that will be vital to your understanding of how to comply with the ISO 9000 Standard and QS-9000 Requirements.

The Memory Jogger™ 9000 is the product of a collaboration between GOAL/QPC and Robert Peach, of Peach and Associates, who is a world-renowned consultant for ISO 9000 and editor of *The ISO 9000 Handbook*. Spiral-bound pocket guide measures 3.5" x 5.5". 1996. 164 pages. ISBN 1-879364-82-4. Code 1060E. $7.95 per copy. Quantity discounts available.

"The ISO/QS-9000 quality game is somewhat new to everybody and a complete, reader-friendly pocket guide is a perfect companion to anyone in the field. This new Memory Jogger™ 9000 is a perfect concept tool to help you implement the ISO 9000 Quality Systems Standard and the Automotive QS-9000 Quality System Requirement."

Lloyd D. Brumfield,
Quality Assurance Engineering Specialist,
ASQC Automotive Division Michigan Quality Council, APX International
Ford Motor Company

The Best-Selling Reference on Total Quality

The Memory Jogger™ II

A Pocket Guide of Tools for Continuous Improvement and Effective Planning

Michael Brassard and Diane Ritter

Fits in your pocket

- Learn how to use the basic Quality Control Tools and the Seven Management & Planning Tools
- Learn how to collect data and formulate solutions
- Streamline inefficient processes
- Manage and plan projects
- Make better, more-informed decisions

This pocket guide describes the use of basic tools for making continuous improvements in your organization. Your teams can become more focused and productive, more skilled in identifying and solving critical problems, tackling key issues, and more effective in planning for data- and consensus-inspired action plans and results.

The Memory Jogger™ II uses a case study example to show you how the tools, when used in combination, can become more powerful and effective for solving problems and reaching goals. It includes examples from well-known organizations in a variety of industries that show how real people have used the tools in their workplaces and why these tools are effective, providing clear, step-by-step illustrations that help you construct, understand, and use each tool. Pocket guide measures 3.5" x 5.5". 1994. 164 pages. ISBN 1-879364-44-1. Code 1030E. $7.95 per copy. Quantity discounts available.

"Thousands of our associates utilize The Memory Jogger™ and
The Memory Jogger Plus+® in our never-ending journey toward a total quality culture…
This new version places all these tools (plus more) together in a useful,
easy-to-read pocket book. It makes the journey just that much easier."

**Don Botto,
Director of Total Quality Culture
The Goodyear Tire & Rubber Co.**

The Team Educator's Best Resource for Teaching . . .

Coach's Guide to The Memory Jogger™ II

The easy-to-use, complete reference for working with improvement and planning tools in teams

Michael Brassard, Diane Ritter, and Others

- Provides a standard, easy-to-use format that allows coaches to find information quickly
- Offers instruction that applies to formal training situations and impromptu learning opportunities
- Helps coaches and teams choose the right tool for the situation
- Covers commonly asked questions about the tools and the process of using and constructing the tools
- Outlines simple examples, learning activities, and step-by-step tips on the construction of each tool
- Presents real company examples and the story behind each team's experience using one or more of the tools

The *Coach's Guide* makes it easier than ever to use *The Memory Jogger™ II* as a key resource in your effective training efforts. You can get your teams to better use the basic quality control tools and management and planning tools so that they can achieve the objectives they've set for themselves and the organization. Most importantly, it gets teams to rely less on the facilitator and more on developing their own self-sufficiency. Tabbed by each chapter for your convenience, the *Coach's Guide* is packed with everything you'll need to better utilize *The Memory Jogger™ II*. 1995. 254 pages. ISBN 1-879364-47-6. Code 1040P. Non-member: $29.95, Member: $26.95. Quantity discounts are available. Call for details.

"The Coach's Guide is far superior to anything we've used in the past. It cuts our training time, which gives the team more time to use the tools in real project situations."
Stewart Davis
Internal Consultant for Excellence!/Customer Satisfaction
NORTEL Northern Telecom